Hiram Hodge

Arizona as it is

The coming country

Hiram Hodge

Arizona as it is
The coming country

ISBN/EAN: 9783337204839

Printed in Europe, USA, Canada, Australia, Japan

Cover: Foto ©Andreas Hilbeck / pixelio.de

More available books at **www.hansebooks.com**

ARIZONA AS IT IS;

OR,

THE COMING COUNTRY.

COMPILED FROM

NOTES OF TRAVEL DURING THE YEARS
1874, 1875, AND 1876.

BY

HIRAM C. HODGE.

NEW YORK:
PUBLISHED BY HURD AND HOUGHTON.
BOSTON : H. O. HOUGHTON AND COMPANY.
Cambridge: The Riverside Press.
1877.

RIVERSIDE, CAMBRIDGE:
STEREOTYPED AND PRINTED BY
H. O. HOUGHTON AND COMPANY.

PREFACE.

WHEN the author entered Arizona, in 1874, he had little thought of being able to gather material for a work on the country. Sick, weak, and debilitated, caused by long years of suffering from bronchial and pulmonary diseases, his greatest hope was to write up descriptive articles of the country for the Press in different sections of the Union. In a few months, the mild, healthful, and pure climate had worked a radical change, giving promise of restored health, and with this change, coupled with the request and solicitation of hundreds of Arizona's best citizens, came the desire to write up in book form whatever might be gathered by a thorough exploration of the Territory. In addition to copies of over five hundred communications published by different newspapers in widely different sections of the United States, a full record was kept day by day of everything seen and learned during his long explorations, a brief account of which is given in these pages. The sole object of the author has been to write a truthful and accurate description of the Territory as it now is, and to give to the public reliable information concerning it. With the wish that this work, though far from complete, may contribute to the development and future prosperity of Arizona, and with unbounded confidence in the future of that great country, it is given to the public, with the hope that it may be read with care and criticised with forbearance.

THE AUTHOR.

TESTIMONIAL.

———◆———

DURING the years 1874, 1875, and 1876, Col. H..C. Hodge has made a thorough tour and exploration of Arizona. His articles on the country, descriptive of its mineral, agricultural, grazing, and other resources, and of its climate, scenery, and prehistoric ruins, published in different sections of the Union, have been truthful, and more full and complete than any heretofore given the public, and believing him to be an honest, truthful, and reliable gentleman, we commend him and his writings and lectures to the people of the United States, with the assurance that full confidence may be given to his reports on Arizona.

ARIZONA, *October*, 1876.

(Signed.)   A. P. K. SAFFORD, Governor A. T.

H. S. STEVENS, Delegate in Congress from A. T.

AUGUST V. KAUTZ, Commanding Military Department of A. T.

F. H. GOODWIN, United States Marshal of A. T.

J. S. VOSBURG, Adjutant General of A. T.

COLES BASHFORD, late Secretary of A. T.

P. R. BRADY, member of Council, A. T.

A. E. DAVIS, member of Council, A. T.

J. P. HARGRAVE, member of Council, A. T.

JOHN G. CAMPBELL, member of Council, A. T.

J. M. REDONDO, member of Council, A. T.

JOHN T. ALSOP, speaker House of Representatives, A. T.

A. L. MOELLER, member House of R., A. T.

C. P. HEAD, member House of R., A. T.

S. R. DE LONG, member House of R., A. T.

SAMUEL PURDY, JR., member House of R., A. T.

JAMES P. BULL, member House of R., A. T.

GIDEON BROOKS, member House of R., A. T.

THOMAS CARDIS, United States Collector Internal Revenue, A. T.

P. R. TULLY, Territorial Treasurer, A. T.

LEVI RUGGLES, Register United States Land Office, Florence, A. T.

M. S. STILES, Receiver Land Office and United States Disbursing Agent, Florence, A. T.

C. H. BRINLEY, United States Deputy Collector of Customs, Yuma, A. T.

T. J. BUTLER, Editor "Miner," Prescott, A. T.

WM. J. BERRY, Editor "Sentinel," Yuma, A. T.

JOHN W. LEONARD, Assistant Editor "Enterprise," Prescott, A. T.

BRIGGS GOODRICH, District Attorney, First District, A. T.

H. B. SUMMERS, District Attorney, Pinal County, A. T.

H. H. CARTER, Judge of Probate, Yavapai County, A. T.

H. N. ALEXANDER, Judge of Probate, Yuma County, A. T.

WILLIAM A. HANCOCK, District Attorney, Maricopa County, A. T.

GEORGE D. KENDALL, Mayor of Prescott, A. T.

C. A. LUKE, Ex-mayor of Prescott, A. T.

EDWARD F. BOWERS, Sheriff, Yavapai County, A. T.

WILLIAM WILKERSON, Clerk of Court and Recorder, Yavapai County, A. T.

H. C. MEADOR, Deputy, Yavapai County, A. T.

S. W. CARPENTER, Recorder, Pima County, A. T.

JOHN J. DIVINE, Recorder, Pinal County, A. T.

O. F. TOWNSEND, Recorder, Yuma County, A. T.

JAY G. KELLY, Assayer, Prescott, A. T.

BLAKE & COMPANY, Prescott, A. T.

And many others.

CONTENTS.

CHAPTER I.

ARIZONA. — HOW ACQUIRED. — ORGANIZATION. — BOUNDARIES
AND EXTENT. — DEFINITION OF NAME, ETC. . . . 13

CHAPTER II.

EARLY SETTLEMENT BY SPANIARDS AND JESUIT PRIESTS. —
OLD MISSIONS, ETC. 17

CHAPTER III.

DESCRIPTION OF THE OLD MISSION CHURCH OF SAN XAVIER
DEL BAC 21

CHAPTER IV.

CLIMATE, RAINY SEASONS, HEALTH, ETC. 27

CHAPTER V.

MOUNTAINS OF ARIZONA: EXTENT, CHARACTER, AND GEN-
ERAL DESCRIPTION 32

CHAPTER VI.

RIVERS OF ARIZONA: SIZE, EXTENT, AND LOCATION . . 35

CHAPTER VII.

AGRICULTURAL AND FARMING LANDS: EXTENT, LOCATION,
ETC. 42

CHAPTER VIII.

GRAZING LANDS. — EXTENT. — STOCK RAISING. — WOOL, ETC. 54

CHAPTER IX.

WOOD, TIMBER, ETC. 57

CHAPTER X.

Mineral Lands: Mines and Mining 61

CHAPTER XI.

Principal Mineral Belts of Arizona. — Remarks and Suggestions 137

CHAPTER XII.

Counties and Towns. — Population, etc. 143

CHAPTER XIII.

Indian Tribes: Locality, Numbers, and General Description 156

CHAPTER XIV.

Prehistoric Ruins of Arizona 177

CHAPTER XV.

Schools and Education 196

CHAPTER XVI.

Railroads, Stage and Post Routes 200

CHAPTER XVII.

Colorado Steam Navigation Company. — History of, and Statistics 208

CHAPTER XVIII.

Newspapers 211

CHAPTER XIX.

Telegraphs 213

CHAPTER XX.

Military, and Military Posts 215

CHAPTER XXI.

Wild Animals, Birds, Fish, etc. 221

CHAPTER XXII.

REPTILES, VENOMOUS INSECTS, ETC. 226

CHAPTER XXIII.

NATURAL CURIOSITIES. — GRAND SCENERY, ETC. . . . 229

CHAPTER XXIV.

THE FLORA OF ARIZONA 242

CHAPTER XXV.

ROUTES OF TRAVEL TO ARIZONA 249

CHAPTER XXVI.

DISTANCES FROM POINT TO POINT 254

CHAPTER XXVII.

REFERENCES FOR INFORMATION AND GENERAL REMARKS ON
EMIGRATION TO ARIZONA 259

CHAPTER XXVIII.

PRICES OF PRODUCE, PROVISIONS, LABOR, ETC. — GENERAL
REMARKS 268

UTAH
ARIZONA
YAVAPAI
NEVADA
Sierra del Carrizo
Navajo Indians
Moquis Pueblos
Painted Desert
Colorado Cañon
Colorado River
North Side Mts
Yampais Village
Colorado Chiquito or Little Colorado Riv.
Head of Navigation
Old Fort
Gold
Mt. Kendrick
Mt. San Francisco
Bill Williams Mt
Mt Sitgreaves
Cedar Forest
Picacho Mt
Music Mt
Cactus Pass
Blue Peaks
Cosnina Indians
Tonto Indians
Yampais Inds.
Aztec Pass
Mt. Hope
Mohave City
Ft. Mohave
Mohave Valley
Cottonwood Valley
Mt Davis
Eldorado
Chimuehueva Valley
Ft. Whipple
PRESCOTT
Yavapai
Weaver
New Mines
Mine Valley
Big Bug
ATLANTIC & PACIFIC
PROPOSED R.R.
Forest
Indians
Navajo Indians
Tune Cha
Forest Lagoons
Snow Spr.
Hualpais Spr.
Aquarius Mts
Chocolate Pool
Colorado Chiquito
Cheveluns Cr.
Beaches Cr.
Camp Lewis
East Fk
Aqua Fria
Settlement
Chimuehuevas
Black Mts
Rapids
Painted Cañon
Hot Spring
Red L.
Laguna
San Francisco Spr.
Salt Spr.
Jacobs Well
Navajo Spr.
Carrizo Spr.
Willow Spr.
White Rock Spr.
Limestone Spr.
Shupaulahwee
Hualpec
Tegua Town
Orayba
Gardens
Cascade Spring
Leroux Spr.
Aspen Spr.
Juniper Spr.
Partridge
Valley de Chino
Whipples Crossing
Aztec Mts
Inscription Spr.
Bill Williams
Santa Maria Cr.
Hassayampa
Turkey Creek
Agua Fria Rancho
Cedar Cr.
Park Cr.
Colorado Cr.
R. del Chelly
Zuni R.
Zuni
Gold
LOS TINTOS

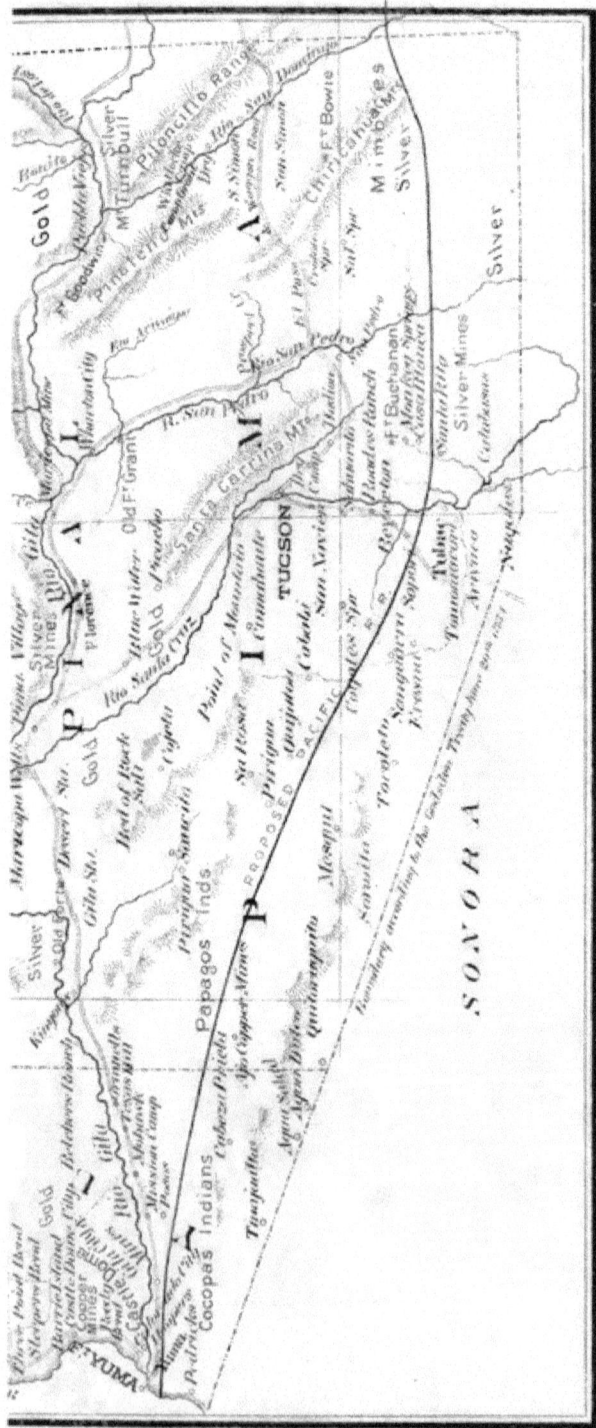

ARIZONA.

CHAPTER I.

HOW ACQUIRED. — ORGANIZATION. — BOUNDARIES AND EXTENT. — NAME.

THAT portion of United States territory known as Arizona, was, prior to the treaty between Mexico and the United States, February 2, 1848, a portion of the Mexican state of Sonora. Owing to a misunderstanding between the two governments respecting the boundary line, another treaty was made in 1854, by which the United States acquired that portion of the territory south of the Gila River, commonly known as the Gadsden Purchase, paying for the same the sum of ten millions of dollars. From this time until 1863, Arizona was appended to New Mexico.

By act of Congress, February 24, 1863, Arizona was formed into a separate and distinct Territory of the United States, and was duly organized by its Governor, the Hon. John N. Goodwin, at Navajoe[1]

[1] Nav-a-ho.

Springs, December 29, 1863. The seat of government was established, by proclamation of the Governor, at or near Fort Whipple, which was then in the beautiful Chino Valley, twenty-two miles north of where Prescott now is. This fort was removed in 1866 to its present location one mile north of Prescott, where the government had been located in 1864. In 1867 the seat of government was removed to Tucson, an old Spanish town in the rich Santa Cruz Valley, some seventy-five miles north of the Sonora line, at which place it still remained in December, 1876, but was removed back to Prescott in January, 1877.

The Hon. Richard C. McCormick came to the Territory with Governor Goodwin and suite as secretary of the Territory, and succeeded Governor Goodwin as governor, and afterwards was delegate in Congress for six years, and was succeeded as delegate by the Hon. Hiram S. Stevens, the present delegate. The Hon. A. P. K. Safford succeeded Governor McCormick as governor, and has held the position for the past six years in an acceptable manner.

Arizona is in latitude 31° 20' to 37° north, and in longitude 32° to 37° 40' west from Washington, and contains about 122,000 square miles, or 78,080,000 acres, the whole area being nearly three times that of the State of New York, and one third larger than all the New England States combined. It is bounded on the north by Nevada and Utah, on the east by New Mexico, on the south by the Mexican state of Sonora, and on the west by California and Nevada.

Of the origin and significance of the name, Arizona, there seems to be much doubt, and a score or more of definitions have been given by different and well-informed persons. Referring back to the old Aztec traditions, the following significant item occurs, which may assist somewhat in the explanation.

" The earth is the offspring of the sky. Long prior to the present race of men, the earth was peopled by a race of giants who in time died off, leaving the earth uninhabited. After a long time, a celestial virgin, a child of one of the thirteen great deities who rule all things, came down to the earth, and being well pleased, remained for a long time its sole inhabitant. Once when in a deep sleep, a drop of dew from heaven fell on her, and she conceived and bore two children, a son and daughter, from whom have sprung all the people of the earth. The name of this celestial virgin was Arizunna, the beautiful, or sun beloved maiden." The Mohave language, which is by far the most perfect and complete of any of the Indian dialects of the country, has two words of nearly the same meaning : Ari, meaning the sun, holy, good, or beautiful ; and Urnia, maid, or maiden ; which together means the land of the beautiful or lovely maiden. This may be the true meaning of the word

Arizona. Another definition is this, Ari, from the Mohave, meaning beautiful, or good, and Zona, from the Spanish, a zone, and taken together, meaning the land of the beautiful zone. Both of these definitions seem to be well made, and both are quite significant and expressive.

CHAPTER II.

EARLY SETTLEMENT BY SPANIARDS, JESUIT PRIESTS, OLD MISSIONS, ETC.

IT has been found very difficult to trace up the history of the first explorations and settlements in what is now the Territory of Arizona. Sufficient has been learned, however, to warrant the assertion, that about thirty years subsequent to the conquest of Mexico by Cortez, or near the year 1551, the early Spanish explorers and the Jesuit Fathers penetrated into this then unknown country. In 1540 a Spanish expedition traversed Northern Sonora, now Arizona and New Mexico.[1] They carried back with them to the city of Mexico wonderful accounts of the country, and of reports gathered from the Indians of the seven wonderful cities of Sibola, which other Spanish expeditions afterwards went in search of, and which are now supposed to have been the seven towns originally built by the Zuñi Indians many hundreds of years since. About the year 1560, a permanent settlement was made by the Spanish explorers and

[1] See Weeeler's Reports and Notes.

2

Jesuit Fathers, at or near where Tucson now is. It
may be mentioned in this connection, that Santa Fé,
New Mexico, was supposed to have been settled in
1555, — Tucson in 1560, and San Augustine, Florida,
in 1565; thus making Santa Fé the first, Tucson the
second, and San Augustine the third settled town
within the present domain of the United States.

One of the oldest missions established by the Jesuit Fathers was that of St. Gertrude de Tabac, in the
Santa Cruz Valley, forty-five miles south of Tucson,
the latter part of the sixteenth century. A writer
in "Rudo Ensayo," in 1762, says, that the Indians
on the San Pedro River state that the missions were
built previous to 1694. Solorano, a Spanish writer
during the reign of Philip III., also mentions these
old missions, and gives much information respecting
the country, the old prehistoric ruins, etc.[1] In the
"Cronica Serifica" of about the same date, a long account is given of the early explorations, the old missions, and of the Indians then in that region, who were
estimated at 75,000.

In 1720, the missions were prosperous and flourish-
ing, and in Sonora, including what is now Arizona,
there were twenty-nine missions and seventy-three
Christian Indian pueblos, or villages, in charge of the
Jesuit Fathers. In what is now Arizona there were
known to have been the missions of San Xavier del

---

[1] See first volume of Solorano, page 218 and on.

Bac, St. Gertrude de Tabac, St. Joseph de Tumaca-Cara, San Miguel de Sonoitag, Guavavi, Calabasas, Arivaca, and Santa Ana. In 1751, there was an outbreak of the Pima and other Indians, who destroyed some of these mission churches, and killed many of the priests in charge. In 1769, the Marquis de Croix, Viceroy of Mexico, sent to the Superior of Santa Cruz in Europe, and had fourteen priests sent out to the New World to fill the places of those killed by the Indians in this outbreak. In 1778, two missions were established on the Colorado River near where Yuma now is, and in 1781 these were destroyed by the Indians and the priests in charge were murdered.

The mission church of St. Augustine at Tucson was founded by one of the priests sent out by request of the Marquis de Croix in 1769, and this old mission church has long been in ruins. The first mission church of San Xavier del Bac was founded at a very old date, — now unknown, — and on its ruins was commenced, in 1768, the present mission church of that name, the only one of all the old missions now standing. It is a model of architecture, and excites the wonder and admiration of all who visit it; and from its antiquity and surroundings, and the many interesting circumstances connected with it, deserves special mention, to which a subsequent chapter will be devoted. Since 1720 to the present date, **1877,** there have **been forty-seven** priests **of the** Jesuit **and** Franciscan orders sent **into** what is **now** Arizona, **of whom more than one half** have **been** murdered **by the** Indians, **or died from** privation **and** suffering.

CHAPTER III.

DESCRIPTION OF THE OLD MISSION CHURCH OF SAN XAVIER DEL BAC.

THE erection of the present mission church of "San Xavier del Bac" was commenced in 1768, on the site of one of the same name which had gone to decay. It is some ten miles south of Tucson, in the rich and beautiful valley of the Santa Cruz, and near the Papago villages. It was completed in 1798, with the exception of one of the towers, which is yet in an unfinished state. Its dimensions are 115×70 feet. The style of architecture is a commingling of the Moorish and the Byzantine. The outside is castellated, and surrounded by one dome and two minarets. The foundation walls are of brick with a fine coating of cement. The outside walls are of brick also cemented. The inside walls are of stone and cement, plastered and stuccoed, and the interior has the form of the Latin cross. The church fronts to the south, and the front centre is covered with beautiful scroll work, having also the coat of arms of the Franciscan monks, which is a cross, with a rope coil above, and two arms below, one of which represents that of Christ, and is naked, the other one that of St. Francis de Assisi, and is partially clothed, St. Francis de Assisi being the patron of the church. A life sized bust of St. Francis Xavier adorned and surmounted the front, but the head and part of the bust have been broken off by some modern Vandal. The roof is surrounded by a brick balustrade cemented, and at each angle and corner are griffons worked in cement, forty-eight in all. On the outside of the church to the west is a wide open niche where the Papago Indians were formerly congregated for morning prayers, and adjoining this, was the old Indian burial ground and dead chapel. Of late years, for sanitary reasons, the dead are buried farther down the valley. To the south of the church are the old convent buildings, which of late have been renovated and occupied by four of the sisters of St. Joseph, who for several years past have lived here teaching a school for the Papago children, and caring for and comforting the sick among the Indians.

When once inside the church, the beholder is forcibly struck with the display of skill in its structure, its beauty and grandeur, and the taste displayed in its adornment. The inside of the church has the form of the Latin cross, the foot being to the south, and extending thence to the north end, where the main altar is. The walls and ceilings are tastefully

decorated and frescoed. The main altar is dedicated
to St. Francis Xavier, and one of the central chapels
to St. Francis de Assisi. Four large fresco paintings
represent the Annunciation, the Visitation of the
Virgin to Elizabeth, the Nativity of Christ, and the
Visitation of the Magi. The altar work, and all
the cornices, are done in cement, as are also the six
arched ceilings overhead, the main one of which is
fifty feet high, and the others about thirty feet high.
The ceilings were all frescoed, but much of this has
been defaced by time, and the elements. The Four
Evangelists, in sculpture, adorn the main altar, and
the scroll work is covered with gold leaf, which in its
early days, when the frescoes and paintings were
fresh and bright, and all the other surroundings new
and in perfect harmony, must have presented a beautiful, grand, and gorgeous sight, especially to the half
wild Indians who had never before seen anything of
like character.

In the lateral chapel of the Virgin, there is a cross
of small pieces of ironwood, imbedded in cement, on
which there was formerly a sculptured figure of
Christ. Within the body of the church there are
in all over fifty pieces of sculpture, most of which
are grand and beautiful, perfect in form, feature, and
position. In two of the angles of the main arch,
there are two most beautiful statues, representing
angels, which tradition states are portraits of the

two daughters of the artist who decorated the church. The main aisle is adorned by two large fresco paintings representing the Last Supper and the Pentecost. The foregoing is but a faint and imperfect description of this old and venerable church, whose wonderful beauty and symmetry of form attracts the attention of all, and creates wonder, surprise, and admiration in the bosom of every beholder. East of the altar, a door leads into the vestry, where the valuables of the church are kept. In former times there were large quantities of gold and silver ornaments, priests' vestments, and other furniture, which was kept in the vestry, some of which has been lost, stolen, or carried away to other churches, and a portion yet remains, among which, are one full set of priests' vestments, two gold cruets of about six ounces each, a large silver cross, several candlesticks of solid silver, a Douay Bible of date 1692, and a few other minor ornaments. On the door leading to the vestry is the name of its builder, Pedro Bojargues, 1797. The masonry work of the church was executed by two brothers named Gauna, who evinced great skill and genius in their work. From the south end of the main aisle, a doorway leads to the west, into the baptismal chapel, and from there a flight of winding stairs, consisting of twenty-seven, twenty-one, and twenty-one steps, leads to the upper floor of the west minaret or tower. At the rise of twenty-seven steps, a doorway leads to the right into the choir gallery, which is arched and frescoed. A further rise of twenty-one steps leads to the second floor of this tower, where there is a chime of four old and rich sounding bells, one of date 1804, and the three others so old and defaced by time, their date is obliterated. From this floor a doorway leads to the roof of the main building, and on going across, the visitor enters the east tower, where but one bell remains of the four formerly there. The date of the one remaining is also obliterated by time, but it carries the mark of some worse than Vandal, who has made of it a rifle target. Returning to the west tower, the visitor rises the last flight of twenty-one steps to the upper floor of the tower, from whence a fine view is obtained of the beautiful valley of the Santa Cruz, of distant mountain chains, of picacho peaks, and many evidences of ancient upheavals and volcanic eruptions. The steps leading to the upper floor, sixty-nine in all, have a rise of ten inches each, making the whole rise fifty-seven and one half feet. When it is remembered that this old, venerable, and wonderful church was commenced one hundred and eight years since, in a wild Indian country, far from the centres of civilization, we can but admire the great energy, perseverance, and indomitable will of the old Jesuit and Franciscan Fathers who planned, carried out, and so successfully accomplished this great work. It is the

only remaining edifice left in the Territory of the
many erected by those of a former century and age,
and should be cared for and preserved by legislative
enactment, as a memento of the past.

CHAPTER IV.

CLIMATE, RAINY SEASONS, HEALTH, ETC.

THE climate of Arizona is varied, embracing every variety, from that of the northern States, to that of the extreme of the sunny south. On the highest mountain peaks, from ten thousand to thirteen thousand feet in height, snow falls to a great depth, and remains on the ground in places from six to ten months of the year. On the mountains, at an altitude of eight thousand feet, the snow fall is two to four feet, and remains from one to three months. At an altitude of six thousand feet, — that of Prescott, — there is a snow fall of a few inches to one foot or more, and the snow remains for a few days only, except in extreme cases, when it has remained for a few weeks only. At this altitude the seasons of spring, summer, and fall, are extremely pleasant, salubrious, and enjoyable, equal to any in the world. The nights are pleasantly cool and agreeable, and two pairs of blankets at night will ever be found to be a necessary covering. At an elevation of four thousand feet, which is that of Mineral Park, Cerbat,

San Carlos, Pueblo Viejo Valley, Camp Grant, and
many other places, there is but little snow fall, the
winters are chilly, but not cold, and the summers
pleasant and delightful, the nights moderately cool,
sufficiently so to give to all a good and refreshing
night's rest. At an altitude of fifteen hundred to
two thousand feet, which is that of the great plains
and valleys of the southern part of the Territory,
Tucson, Florence, Phœnix, etc., snow is almost
wholly unknown, the winters are extremely mild
and pleasant, and the summers warm and dry, with
continued warm weather for many months. At this
altitude the climate in summer, though quite warm,
is not oppressive, or debilitating, as in many other
parts of our country with the same range of thermometer, 85° to 105°. Owing to the pure and rarefied condition of the atmosphere, and the cool nights,
the human system keeps in a healthy tone. At lower
altitudes, especially at Yuma, which has an elevation
of but one hundred and sixty feet above tide water,
the thermometer often runs up to 110°, and in extreme cases to over 120°, yet at Yuma, cases of sun-
stroke are unknown, and its citizens enjoy most excellent health. From the foregoing, it will be noticed
that the altitude of the country gives the different
degrees and variety of temperature.

There is probably no country in the world with a
purer, healthier climate than Arizona, and the sick,

the debilitated, the worn out and enfeebled constitutions of other climes and countries, can here find a climate of exceeding purity, ranging through all the degrees from hot to cold, according to altitude, from which each and every one can select that locality in summer, or winter, that is required by their constitution or ailments. For consumptives and those having kindred diseases, the winter climate of Yuma, and thence east to Maricopa Wells, Phœnix, Florence, and Tucson, and especially at Yuma, there is no more favorable climate in the known world, and when the country is opened up, and traversed by railroads, Yuma and the other points named will of necessity become the centres of sanitariums of world-wide celebrity. In summer, the mountainous regions are equally favorable for like diseases, and also for all asthmatic and respiratory diseases. The worst cases of asthma are invariably cured by a residence in the mountains of Arizona of a few months.

There are two rainy seasons each year in the Territory, one of which is usually the months of February and March, and the other the months of July and August, but these rainy seasons sometimes come earlier and sometimes later. Occasionally they will continue for three and four months, and some years there is a rain-fall during every month, more especially in the mountains. The amount of rain-fall differs much in different localities of the Territory, being far greater in the mountains than in the great plains and valleys. In the mountains it ranges from twelve to thirty or more inches, and in the plains and valleys from one to twelve inches. At Yuma the rain-fall has in some years been less than one inch, but this is exceptional, the usual quantity being from three to five inches. The sky here during the whole year is almost invariably a clear, blue expanse of ether. The extreme purity of the atmosphere, and the almost continued and perpetual sunshine which pervades the Territory, has attracted the attention of every observing person who has been there either for a few months, or for years. The author made a special note of the fact, that during his residence there of over two years, there was never, not in all that time, in summer or winter, one single day without bright, beautiful sunshine. There is perhaps no other country which presents this peculiarity in so marked a manner, where there is any rain-fall at all. The rain clouds do not overspread the whole heavens as in the Atlantic States, but pass over in areas of narrow width, following up the mountain spurs and chains, and often, when the rain-fall upon a mountain top, or mountain plateau, is sufficient to transform the tiny rivulet, or mountain brooklet, into a raging torrent of waters, there will be in the valley below, only a few miles distant, continued sunshine, a balmy and fragrant atmosphere, and continued employment for man and beast.

It is a grand and glorious sight to witness a thunder-storm in the mountains of Arizona, to listen to the rolling, rumbling, almost deafening reverberations of the thunder, as the thunder-cloud passes over some lofty mountain plateau, or hangs along the crest of some jagged mountain cliff, and witness the vivid play of the forked lightning, as it flashes from cloud to cloud, or darts meteor like from crag to crag; while during this time, the observer is basking in the sunshine in some beautiful valley just outside the mountain range, where all nature is pleasant, quiet, and serene.

CHAPTER V.

MOUNTAINS OF ARIZONA: EXTENT, CHARACTER, ETC.

ARIZONA is properly a mountainous country, though there are great plains and valleys in the country, more especially in its southern part. The mountainous districts cover about two thirds of the Territory, and the great plains and valleys about one third.

The main mountain chains are the White, Mogollon, San Francisco, Bill Williams, Pinal, Apache, Cerbat, Juniper, Hualapai, Bradshaw, Peacock, Music, Mazatsal, Santa Catarina, Santa Teresa, Santa Rita, Patagonia, Dragoon, Chiricahua, Graham, Antelope, Cordilleras de Gila, Sierra Ancha, Hacquahilla, besides many others of less note, and small detached spurs, or picacho peaks, generally with local names. The highest peak of San Francisco mountain is 13,000 feet. It is some eighty-five miles a little east of north from Prescott, and is the highest mountain in the Territory. Its northern declivities are covered with snow for ten months in the year. The highest peak of the White Mountains, called by the Spanish and Mexicans the " Sierra Blanco " Mountains, is 12,000 feet high, that of the Bill Williams and Union Peak, 10,000, and Mount Graham 8,000 feet. Several others are from 8,000 to 10,000 feet in height. Many of the mountain peaks are noted landmarks, and can be seen for long distances. That of San Francisco, the mountain monarch of all the mountains of Arizona, whose rockribbed summits are ancient as the sun, can be seen in different directions for two hundred miles. The Four Peaks, near camp McDowell, can be seen for over one hundred miles, and Castle Dome in the Colorado River range, nearly the same distance. This noted landmark will be more fully described in a subsequent chapter. Superstition Mountain, thirty miles east of Phœnix, is so named from some superstitious traditions of the Indians respecting its being the abode of evil spirits. The " Dos Cabasas " peaks — two heads — in the northern spurs of the Chiricahua Mountains, one hundred miles east from Tucson, are noted landmarks and can be seen for a long distance throughout all of Southeastern Arizona. Their two bald summits look in the distance like the giant heads of some monstrous Titan of old. The peak of Babaquivora, one hundred miles or more to the southwest from Tucson, is another noted landmark.

3

The summits of many of the mountain ranges, especially in the northern portion of the Territory, are wide, level plateaus, covered generally with a splendid growth of pine, spruce, fir, juniper, cedar, and other timber, with clear sparkling mountain springs bursting out at short intervals, at which points there are generally open plats of ground nearly destitute of timber, but covered with a rich coating of wild clover and other nutritious grasses, and reminding one of the beautiful oases in great deserts. These mountain plateaus are well supplied with game, such as bear, deer, antelope, wild turkeys, and in a few places with elk, and also a variety of smaller game.

CHAPTER VI.

RIVERS OF ARIZONA: SIZE, EXTENT, ETC.

THE principal rivers of Arizona are the Colorado, Gila, Salt, Chiquito Colorado, or Little Colorado, Verde, Bill Williams, San Pedro, Santa Cruz, White, Black, and some others of lesser note, which are mostly branches of the main rivers. Many of the mountain streams, which in Arizona are called rivers, would in most other parts of the United States be called creeks, brooks, or rivulets.

The great Colorado River is formed by the Green and Grand rivers, and other streams far to the north. The Grand River rises in Colorado, in the western declivities of the Rocky Mountains, and runs a southwesterly course to its junction with the Green. The Green rises far up in Wyoming, near Fremont's Peak, and runs a southerly course to where it unites with the Grand, in Utah, from which point of union it is called the Colorado. The Colorado is navigable for steamers of four hundred tons at all seasons of the year, as far as Hardyville, five hundred and thirteen miles above its mouth, and steamers have been as far

up as Callville, six hundred and forty-one miles from
the Gulf of California. From its mouth to the foot
of the Grand Cañon, a distance of seven hundred
miles, the river at low water has an average width
of about six hundred feet, and a depth of five to
twenty feet. From the extreme head waters of its
upper branches, the Colorado River has a total length
including its windings of some three thousand miles,
and it is the largest and longest river that enters the
Pacific Ocean, south of the Sacramento River, on the
American continent. The Colorado River region
presents some of the grandest scenery on the globe.
For nearly three hundred miles, in Northern Arizona,
its waters, during the untold ages of the past, have
worn through great mountain chains, and mountain
plateaus, cutting out for itself a channel many hundreds and thousands of feet deep in the hard granite,
slate, porphyry, sandstone, limestone, and volcanic
rocks, thus forming the Grand Cañon of the Colorado,
the grandest cañon the eye of man ever saw. This
cañon can in no way be fully explored, except by entering it with boats from its upper part in Utah, as
Lieutenant Powell and party did, in 1869 ; and then
it is a Herculean task, requiring a large degree of energy, perseverance, and indomitable courage. For a
full description of this wonderful cañon, the reader is
referred to Major Powell's reports of his expedition
down the river, all of which will be found exceedingly

interesting in its description of the scenery, and of
hair-breadth escapes from dangers and death, which
exceed in interest the wildest imaginations of the
most fertile brain. Many lateral cañons enter the
main one, in its long and tortuous course, all of exceeding interest to the admirers of the grand and sublime in nature. Between the Grand Cañon, where it
opens out from its rocky inclosure, down to Yuma,
there are several other deep, abysmal cañons, from
five to twenty miles long, through which the great
volume of waters of the Colorado, collected from a
thousand mountain streams, rush with whirlpool ve-
locity, bearing onward, ever onward, in its mass of
waters, a thick sediment of alluvium, which is deposited along its banks, and in the upper portion of the
Gulf of California, adding year after year large tracts
of rich alluvial land to the tens of thousands of acres
heretofore deposited by the river in the long eras of
the past.

The Gila River, the largest tributary of the Colorado, rises far to the east in New Mexico to the northeast of Silver City, pursues a general westerly course,
enters Arizona near the rich Clifton Copper Mines,
passing through the beautiful Pueblo Viejo Valley,
the San Carlos Indian Agency, and the mountains
below, and emerging into the lower, or great Gila
Valley, some twelve miles above Florence, the county
town of Pinal County, and thence west for nearly

three hundred miles to its junction with the Colorado
at Yuma. The total length of the Gila, including its
many windings, is fully six hundred and fifty miles.
For four hundred miles, at low water, the Gila has
an average width of about one hundred feet, and a
depth of one to two feet.

Salt River rises well up towards the eastern part
of the Territory, in the White Mountains, its head
waters being the White and Black rivers. It has
numerous large branches, coming in mostly from the
north, draining the country far to the north, including the Tonto Basin, the Sierra Ancha, White, San
Francisco, and other mountains. Its course is west
and southwest, and it unites with the Gila below
Phœnix some thirty miles. This river was named
the "Rio Salido," by the early Spanish and Jesuit
explorers, on account of its waters being highly impregnated with salt, which is easily noticed at low
water. This is caused by a heavy salt formation
through which the river passes about one hundred
miles above Phœnix. At low water it is a clear,
beautiful stream, having an average width of two
hundred feet for a distance of one hundred miles
above its junction with the Gila, and a depth of two
feet or more.

The Verde River is one of the largest northern
branches of Salt River, its upper branches rising at
different points to the east, north, and northwest

from Prescott. It becomes a fine river of eighty feet
in width about fifty miles northeast from Prescott,
and thence runs a southerly course to its junction
with Salt River near Camp McDowell. Its whole
course is about one hundred and fifty miles. The
Tonto, Sipicue, Cherry, Agua Frio, and other large
creeks, are also tributaries of Salt River, coming in
from the north. The main upper branches of Salt
River, the White and Black rivers, are both swift
running mountain streams, and rise in the White
Mountains. They are well stocked with the real
speckled mountain trout, affording rare sport to the
followers and devotees of Izaak Walton.

The Little, or Chiquito Colorado, which has by
some been called Flax River, rises in the northeastern declivities of the White Mountains, near the line
between Arizona and New Mexico, runs in a north-
westerly direction, and enters the main Colorado
in Northern Arizona, about fifty miles south of the
southern line of Utah, and near the head of the
Grand Cañon. The lower part of the Chiquito Colorado runs through a cañon second only to that of the
Grand Cañon of the main Colorado.

Bill Williams Fork is an eastern branch of the Colorado, with which it unites at Aubrey, 235 miles
above Yuma. Its different branches rise, some in
the mountains fifty miles southwest from Prescott,
some near Mount Hope, and some in the Hualapai

Mountains in Mohave County. In its whole course
it is not far from one hundred and fifty miles long,
which is about the same as the Chiquito Colorado.
The Santa Maria is its main eastern branch, and the
Sandy its main northern. These two streams unite
some fifteen miles south from Greenwood, from which
point the Bill Williams Fork flows west to its junction with the Colorado.

The San Pedro rises near the line between Arizona
and Sonora, and runs a general northerly course a
distance of over one hundred miles, and enters the
Gila River near old Camp Grant.

The Santa Cruz River rises also near the Arizona
and Sonora line, southeast from the Patagonia Moun
tains, making a long detour into Sonora to the southwest, thence to the north into Arizona, and finally
sinking in the great plain or valley some twelve
miles to the north from Tucson. The whole length
of the Santa Cruz is not far from one hundred and
fifty miles, to the point where its waters finally sink.
It must have formerly run far to the northwest and
perhaps entered the Gila River below Maricopa
Wells, as its old bed is now distinguishable at different places. One fact connected with most of the
mountain streams of Arizona, and which is applica-
ble to most of the streams west of the Rocky Mountains, is this: The volume of water in the mountains
is much greater than in the valleys and plains below,

which is principally owing to the character of the soil, — generally a disintegrated granite, which is open and porous, permitting the waters to sink in, and percolate through it to a great depth, — and, to a less extent, to evaporation in a dry and hot climate. Some of the larger rivers, such as the Gila, are at times during extreme hot and dry weather dry in their beds for many miles, rising and sinking at intervals as the bed rock comes near the surface. Nearly all of the smaller streams that enter the great valleys and plains present this peculiarity.

The Colorado River drains the western and extreme northern parts of the Territory, the Chiquito Colorado the northeastern part, the Gila and Salt Rivers the central part east and west, and the San Pedro and Santa Cruz the southern part of the Territory.

CHAPTER VII.

AGRICULTURAL AND FARMING LANDS. — EXTENT, LOCATION, ETC.

THE amount of rich agricultural and farming land in the Territory of Arizona is from fifteen to twenty million acres, but owing to a scarcity of water for irrigation, there is now susceptible of cultivation but about two million eight hundred thousand acres. Crops cannot be successfully raised in most of the great valleys and plains without irrigation, and as there is not sufficient water in the rivers, owing to the sinking of the water as before stated, a large portion of them lie waste, and must continue in that state until water is obtained by artesian wells or otherwise, for the purpose, which it is confidently believed will be accomplished most successfully, when the necessities of the country require and demand it.

A splendid opportunity is here presented for action by the General Government, in developing artesian wells at different points in the Territory, thus bringing large quantities of as rich land into market, and under successful cultivation, as can be found on the continent, and aiding at a comparatively trifling expense in the development of the Territory. Many millions of acres of land, now almost worthless and unproductive, would become centres of rich and extensive farming districts, a good population would be introduced, and churches and schools would spring up as if by magic, where now there is no inducement for industrious white people to settle. Government would be repaid a hundred fold by sales of land, and by a wonderful increase in taxable property for the support of government.

This subject has been presented to Congress by the Honorable R. C. McCormick, but it has never received the attention which it deserves. This may be in part owing to indifference, and partly to a lamentable ignorance on the part of our law makers at Washington, respecting the wonderful capacities of this far off and almost isolated Territory. It is to be hoped that future delegates in Congress from the Territory will, among other important matters of legislation, press this one to a successful issue.

The largest tract of agricultural land which can now be cultivated in Arizona, is that on Salt River, in Maricopa County, in and around Phœnix for a distance of from twenty to fifty miles. The amount of such land in this rich valley is approximately one million of acres. The soil is a rich alluvium, capable of producing, with good tillage, twenty-five to fifty bushels of wheat, barley, and corn, to the acre. Beans, melons, pumpkins, sweet potatoes, and other roots and vegetables of most kinds, grow and produce well. Peaches, pears, nectarines, apricots, and all the smaller fruits, also grapes, and most of the semi-tropical fruits can be cultivated with success. Sugar-cane, hemp, tobacco, and no doubt rice and cotton, could also be successfully cultivated.

In the Gila Valley, extending from above Florence to Yuma, there are in all at least five hundred thousand acres of land, similar in character and productiveness to that of the valley of Salt River, and capable of producing the same cereals, vegetables, fruits, etc. In this great valley is the Gila River Indian Reservation, where the Pima Indians have cultivated wheat, corn, pumpkins, melons, etc., for the past two centuries.

In the Chiquito Colorado Valley, including its tributary and lateral valleys, there are about five hundred thousand acres of good farming and grass land, which produces wheat, barley, corn, and most of the fruits and vegetables common to the Northern States. Wild flax grows here very abundantly, and when first explored it was from that reason called Flax River. Many thousand tons of wild hay, of excellent quality, could be cut in this valley annually, and in the course of time this will become very valuable. In the upper part of the valley, at the Milligan Settlement, there is quite a prosperous town springing up, and also at several other favorable points, small villages are starting into active life. Colonies of Mormons have been settling in the lower portions of the valley the past two years, and being an industrious people, will soon become successful colonies.

Along the upper portions of Salt River, including the valleys of its many tributaries, there are in all at least two hundred thousand acres of land, capable of raising most of the products before named, and in those valleys which extend well up into the mountains, Irish potatoes of an excellent quality can be successfully raised.

The Pueblo Viejo Valley, sometimes called the Upper Gila Valley, has, with its tributary valleys, that of Ash Creek and others, over one hundred thousand acres of choice farming land, rich, beautiful, and productive, and is one of the most desirable places for settlement in the whole Territory. Its altitude is about four thousand feet, which is a sufficient elevation to escape the extreme heat of the lower valleys, and to give a mild and healthy climate in winter. Snow is almost unknown in the valley, and the Gila River furnishes a large volume of water sufficient to irrigate most of the valleys when properly distributed. The products are about the same as those of the valleys of the Salt and Gila rivers mentioned above.

On the Arizona side of the Colorado River, there

are in all over one hundred thousand acres of exceedingly rich land, a portion of which is included in the Colorado River Indian Reservation, where the Mohave Indians, and a few from other tribes, have for years past raised considerable quantities of wheat, corn, beans, pumpkins, melons, etc. Wild hemp of an excellent quality grows in many places along the Colorado bottom, and in process of time must become a productive industry. Alfalfa has been grown successfully by Mr. Smith, between Camp Mohave and Hardyville. Rice, cotton, sugar-cane, and tobacco, could be raised along the Colorado successfully. One serious difficulty connected with farming in the Colorado Valley is the constantly changing channel of the river, but when the necessity arrives, means will no doubt be devised to control its waters and confine them in a permanent channel.

There are in the Santa Cruz Valley, and its tributaries, about one hundred thousand acres of choice farming land, a portion of which, near Tucson, has been cultivated continuously for two centuries or more, and is now seemingly as productive as when the valley first became well known to our people, twenty-five years since. In this valley were some of the first settlements of the early Spanish explorers, and here also were located some of the first of the old Jesuit missions founded during the latter part of the sixteenth and the first part of the seventeenth century.

The San Pedro Valley is about fifty miles east from Tucson, in which, and the lateral valleys, are about fifty thousand acres of good farming land, most of which can be successfully cultivated. At Tres Alimos, in this valley, are some well cultivated farms and one choice dairy farm, that of H. C. Hooker, Esq. Near the upper part of the San Pedro Valley is one old Spanish-Mexican land grant, said to be the only one in the Territory which is legal and valid. At Tres Alimos, a grant was made of several leagues many years since, on conditions which were never fulfilled, and consequently the grant is void. This freedom from land grants in Arizona is extremely favorable to its settlement, and its future prosperity and freedom from litigation and strife, which has been so prolific a source of trouble in California. It will give to the settler peace and security, it will give permanent homes to the many, and build up good communities where schools and churches can be supported by a resident and independent farming community.

In the valley of Bill Williams Fork, and along its tributaries, the Sandy, Santa Maria, and other creeks, there are many tracts of excellent farming lands, in all many thousand acres. These tracts are mostly in Mohave County, and embrace nearly all the tillable land in the valleys of that county which are at present supplied with water. There are large valleys,

however, in the county, such as the Sacramento and
Hualapai valleys, which have a rich soil, but no
water to irrigate until artesian water is obtained,
when they would support a population of thousands.
On the summit of the mountains, and the table or
mesa lands, there are many places where potatoes
and other vegetables grow well. One of these localities is on the summit of the Hualapai Mountains,
where Mr. Shoulters has raised large crops of potatoes for several years; and several other localities
could be mentioned.

In Yavapai County there are scores of smaller valleys than those heretofore mentioned, containing from
a few hundred to several thousand acres of choice
land each, where wheat, corn, vegetables of all kinds,
all the common northern fruits, and excellent potatoes can be raised most successfully. In the aggregate
there are in these valleys over one hundred thousand
acres of good land, and these beautiful and pleasant
valleys have a certain charm about them, which is
drawing to them scores of families who are building
up pleasant homes, and happy firesides. The pure
mountain atmosphere which surrounds all the little
valleys in the mountainous regions of Arizona is
drawing to them a large share of the present farming immigration to the Territory, and especially of
families from many of the States and Territories.

The most prominent of these small valleys in

Yavapai County are the Verde, Williamsons, Peeples, Kirkland, Chino, Skull, Agua Frio, Walnut Grove, Walnut Creek, Beaver Creek, and scores of others, which are now being settled up and improved.

Go where one will in all parts of the Territory, in the foot hills, and through the mountains, pleasant and delightful valleys are continually attracting the attention of the explorer, many of them having springs of clear, crystal water, and often one will find small rills and rivulets which are sufficient to supply the wants of many horses, cattle, and sheep.

There evidently was a time in the long past when there was far more running water in Arizona than now, when many of the large valleys, now destitute, were well supplied. Climatic changes, the filling of the valleys to a great depth by a rich alluvium brought down from the mountains by water erosion, and perhaps other causes, have operated to make them as we now find them, destitute of water, and consequently uninhabitable, until water shall be obtained by artesian wells, or otherwise. Could these great valleys and plains be supplied with sufficient water for irrigation, many million acres of exceedingly rich land could be brought under successful cultivation, and would add millions of wealth to the agricultural products of the Territory.

In passing over the great Pacific Mail Stage Line, between Yuma on the Colorada River, and the Steins

4

Peak range of mountains on the east line of the Territory, several of the great valleys and plains are crossed which extend south from the valley of the Gila and along the stage route, and which extend south far down into Sonora a distance of one hundred miles or more.

The Sulphur Springs Valley, seventy-five miles east of Tucson, is from ten to twenty-five miles wide and one hundred miles or more in length, having a rich soil, which with a good water supply would support a large population, but which is now almost entirely worthless for farming purposes, as it is almost wholly destitute of water, except what is obtained from a series of springs at different points in the valley. These springs afford a water supply sufficient for thousands and tens of thousands of cattle, horses, sheep, etc., but not sufficient for farm irrigation.

It is stated that some fifty or more years since, a wealthy Spaniard had a herd of sixty thousand head of cattle in this valley.

To the east of Apache Pass is the San Simon Valley, which is similar to the Sulphur Springs Valley, and of about the same extent and quality. This valley extends north from the line of the Pacific Mail Stage Line to the Pueblo Viejo Valley on the upper Gila River some fifty miles, and south down into Sonora. The soil, like that of the other valleys in the Territory, is exceedingly rich, and like them, owing to the absence of water, almost useless at present for agricultural purposes. There are not over a dozen settlers in these two great valleys, where there might be thousands, if a water supply could be obtained.

A small expenditure of money by the General Government, in developing artesian water here, would be productive of grand results.

Another great plain is between Florence and Phœnix, which covers an area of fifty or more square miles, but differing from the two last mentioned in some respects, being a slightly elevated plateau, or mesa land, at an elevation of one or two hundred feet above the bottom lands of the Gila and Salt rivers; the Gila River being on the south, and Salt River on the north.

Much of this level and beautiful mesa was evidently cultivated by the ancient prehistoric race, who long, long ago, inhabited and cultivated most of the great valleys and plains of Arizona, and who have left here, as elsewhere, many mementoes of their former life, and of their habits, character, and pursuits.

In Mohave County, in the northwestern part of the Territory, there are several great valleys worthy of mention. One of these, the Sacramento Valley, extends from Bill Williams Fork on the south, to Stone's Ferry on the north, a distance of over one hundred and fifty miles, with a width of five to twenty-five miles. This great valley is also destitute of water for irrigation, and without an inhabitant. The soil is rich, and capable of producing an abundant supply of grain, fruits, vegetables, etc., if water could be obtained for irrigation. There is strong evidence that this valley was, at some very remote age, the bed of the Colorado River. It is at no one point over thirty or forty miles east from the Colorado River, and runs nearly parallel with it from Stone's Ferry on the north to the Needles on the southwest, where a portion of the valley enters the Colorado. With an abundant supply of artesian water, this valley would also become a rich and prosperous farming country, and make homes for thousands of industrious tillers of the soil.

Another fine and beautiful valley lies to the east of the Cerbat Mountains, and is known as the Hualapai (wal-la-pi) Valley. It is hemmed in by lofty mountains, the Hualapai Mountains on the south, the Peacock range on the east, the Cerbat range on the west, and the Music Mountains on the north. The valley is eighty miles long nearly north and south, and five to twenty miles wide east and west. There is no permanent stream of water running through this valley, and no outlet for a river if there was any. During the rainy season, the water which falls in the valley, and on the surrounding mountains, is collected into a small lake in its northern part, where it remains for a few months, until carried

off by evaporation, or by seepage into the earth.
This water reservoir is called Red Lake.

In the mountains and foot hills contiguous to, and
surrounding all of these great plains and valleys,
there are many springs and small rivulets, where a
good water supply can be obtained for horses, cattle,
and sheep, but these waters all sink soon after entering the plains and valleys.

There are scores of smaller valleys in different portions of the Territory, somewhat similar in character
to those mentioned, most of which will no doubt in
time be utilized and made productive by means of
artesian wells. Many of these smaller valleys are
now being located and settled on by immigrants from
all parts of the Union, and are being improved to
some extent, especially in the mountain region, where
much of the soil can be successfully cultivated without irrigation.

CHAPTER VIII.

GRAZING LANDS. — EXTENT. — STOCK RAISING. — WOOL, ETC.

THE larger portion of Arizona is emphatically a grazing and stock raising country, and is capable of supporting and fattening an immense number of cattle and sheep. There are but few localities in the whole Territory destitute of rich and nutritive grasses, and at least forty million acres of land is fully equal for grazing, to any on the continent, all of which is well supplied with water conveniently near to the stock ranges.

The wild grasses of the country are very nutritious, embracing varieties of the wild clover, wild barley and oats, black, white, and curly gramma grass, sacatone, six week grass, many varieties of bunch grass, etc., etc.

The mountains, foot hills, and rolling lands, are literally covered with a velvety green for most of the year, and having two rainy seasons, the hills and mountain sides do not present that bleak and barren appearance so characteristic of California scenery for many months of the year. The excellent grazing qualities of Arizona have already attracted the attention of stock men of the contiguous States and Territories, and during the past year many thousands of horses, cattle, and sheep have been taken to the Territory from California, Oregon, Nevada, New Mexico, Texas, and other places. The number of sheep in the Territory is now nearly two million, yet they are scarcely noticed, so extensive is the range.

Arizona is destined at no distant day to become one of the most successful wool producing sections of the Union, and when railroads traverse the country, and connect it with San Francisco and other cities on the Pacific slope, and with St. Louis, Chicago, New Orleans, and other cities east, the rich beef and mutton, from a thousand hills and valleys in Arizona, will be supplied to those markets at reasonable rates, and her wool, free from burrs and other impurities, will be eagerly sought for by the great manufactories of the older States. The climate of Arizona is so mild that when sheep and cattle become well acclimated, there is but little necessity for protection from storm or wind. The mountain ranges of the Territory are extremely favorable to stock raising, and as there are numerous springs and rivulets there, those localities are at present the most favorable points for location. The grasses in the great

valleys, especially in the southeastern part of the
Territory, are very abundant, and where water can be
had, they afford splendid ranges for stock of all
kinds.

The section of country watered by the Chiquito
Colorado River is especially favorable for sheep raising, as is also the region of country around Prescott,
and thence to the north in the region of country
around the San Francisco and Bill Williams mountains. The same can also be said of the country
south of Tucson, embracing the country around the
Santa Rita, Patagonia, Huachuca, Whetstone, Dragoon, and Chiricahua mountains, and in the contiguous valleys. There is no employment more healthful, pleasant, or profitable than stock raising, and for
young men of good habits, combined with watchful-
ness, care, and energy, there is no surer road to
competence and wealth than this. It also offers fine
inducements to those having debilitated constitutions,
and to those broken down in health, to engage in
a business which requires constant out-door exercise,
either on foot or on horseback, in a climate clear,
pure, and exhilarating, where in a few years health
can be fully restored, and a fortune accumulated.

Too much cannot be said of the future prospects
of Arizona in this respect, all of which will be fully
verified in a few short years.

CHAPTER IX.

WOOD, TIMBER, ETC.

A MISTAKEN idea has heretofore prevailed respecting the wood and timber supply of the Territory, which was, that it was almost entirely destitute of a supply for the ordinary wants of the inhabitants. By a thorough exploration of the Territory the author found many large forests of pine, spruce, fir, juniper, cedar, oak, mesquit, with a fair supply of other wood and timber, such as ash, black walnut, poplar, cottonwood, palo verde, alder, willow, etc., etc.

In Arizona, as elsewhere in southern climates, the altitude generally indicates the different varieties of wood and timber which may be looked for. Along the low river bottoms the cottonwood, willow, etc., are found, and on the plains, mesas, and valleys, below four thousand feet altitude, the mesquit, palo verde, and other kindred varieties flourish, and at about four thousand feet, in the foot hills and ravines leading into the mountains, the oak, ash, black walnut, etc., flourish. From four to seven thousand feet altitude the juniper, cedar, Piñon pine, etc., are found, and from five to ten thousand feet, pine, spruce, and fir, arc found in great abundance. A large portion of Northern Arizona is an elevated plateau, from five to eight thousand feet in altitude, most of which is covered with grand forests of pine, spruce, fir, juniper, and cedar. These forests are sufficient in extent to supply all the wants of the Territory for generations, if judiciously used and properly cared for.

The great timber belts include the White, Mogollon, San Francisco, Bill Williams, and other ranges in the northeastern and northern portions of the Territory; the Bradshaw, and contiguous mountains around Prescott, Mount Hope, Hualapai, Music, Cerbat, and other mountain chains to the west, and running through Mohave County; the Pinals, Apache, and contiguous mountains in Maricopa and Pinal counties; Mount Graham, Santa Teresa, Santa Catarina, Chiricahua, Santa Rita, and other mountains in Pima County, and also other timber belts on the different river ranges and mountain spurs in different parts of the Territory, aggregating in all about twenty million acres of timber land.

When the thirty-fifth parallel railroad is built across the continent, it will pass through Arizona to the north of Prescott, and will open up some of the finest bodies of timber on the continent, consisting mostly of the pine and juniper varieties. The forests of juniper will furnish large quantities of the most durable railroad ties, fencing posts, etc., etc. ; and the grand old pine forests will all be needed in process of time for building purposes, mining, and a thousand other wants.

The Texas Pacific, or thirty-second parallel railroad, will open up the timber belts along the Gila River, to the east of Florence in the Pinal, Santa Catarina, Santa Teresa, Mount Graham, and the Chiricahua mountain ranges, on and near which line there are many fine bodies of pine, juniper, and other varieties of timber.

The mesquit, of which there are two varieties, is quite common throughout the Territory below an altitude of four thousand feet. It is a very hard, solid wood, fully equal to hickory for fire-wood, and produces the true gum arabic of commerce, which exudes from the tree similar to the gum of the common cherry tree. It also produces a bean which is eaten both in a green and dry state by the Indians, and which has a pleasant sweetish taste. Its fattening qualities are excellent, and stock of all kinds being fond of the bean, will fatten on it in a few weeks. The largest growth of the mesquit is found in the valley of the Santa Cruz, south of Tucson, and at different points in the Gila and Colorado River valleys.

One variety produces a bean-pod somewhat similar to the Lima bean, or the common string bean of northern gardens, and the other being in form something like a mass or bunch of common screws, is called the screw bean. The Indians collect large quantities of both varieties, which when dried they grind into flour on their metat stones; this they mix with water and drink it for food, living on it for weeks at a time. It makes a nutritious and palatable drink.

The Piñon pine, which grows along the lower line of the large pine forests, and is intermixed with the juniper forests, is excellent for fire-wood, and some other purposes, and produces the Piñon pine nut in great quantities, which is quite an article of diet among the Indians, and is also relished by the whites.

The great bodies of the pine forests of Arizona are as yet untouched by the woodman's axe, and must remain so to a great extent until railroads open up the country, and hasten the time of great improvements and general prosperity to the country. Lumbering has been carried on for some years at Prescott, and a few other places, but the great timber belts are yet untouched.

CHAPTER X.

MINERAL LANDS, MINES AND MINING.

THE mines of Arizona, varied and numberless, are no doubt the sources of the future wealth of the Territory, and consist of gold, silver, copper, lead, iron, coal, salt, and perhaps of other valuable minerals. These mines, especially those of the precious metals, and of copper and lead, are of wonderful extent and richness, and are destined at no distant day to astonish the world by the immensity of their product.

A full description of the different mineral belts of the country, of the locations made, and of the mines already opened, would fill volumes, and therefore will not be attempted in this work. An outline and partial description alone can be given, leaving the subject to be fully written up in the future by some one having more time, and more competent to the task.

Mines of gold and silver were known to exist in what is now Arizona two hundred years or more since, and some successful workings were carried on by the old Jesuit priests, who first explored the Territory, and who employed Mexican and Indian laborers.

After the whole of the Territory came into the possession of the United States, by the Gadsden Purchase in 1854, old mountaineers, trappers, and traders, in their expeditions through the Territory, reported from time to time the discovery of placer gold, but not until about 1860 was there any systematic or continued effort made to locate and work the mines. Reports from time to time reached California, and other mining sections, and in 1862 and 1863 many old miners from California and elsewhere visited the country, and made valuable discoveries of placer diggings. Previous to this, some twenty years since, rich placer diggings were discovered at Gila City, eighteen miles east of Yuma, and at one time a mining population of over three thousand were collected at that point, consisting of whites, Mexicans, and Indians. For a few years mining was a success at that point, and large amounts of the precious metal were taken out, aggregating, as the best informed claim, some two or three millions of dollars.

As in most rich mining localities, a large majority of the miners spent their earnings in riotous living, gambling, and debauchery, and but few of the many saved their fortunes. Owing to a want of water, these placers were after a few years almost deserted, yet a few Mexicans and Indians work at them from time to time, making fair wages. There is no doubt but the placers would pay well now, could water for sluicing or hydraulic washing be obtained at not too great an outlay of capital. The project of bringing water into the diggings from the Gila River has been mooted, and should it be carried out successfully, these placers will again attract large numbers of people.

Some rich placers were discovered and worked some fifteen miles above Yuma, at what was called the Pot-holes, and at the Cienega, where large quantities of gold were taken out for a few years, but these mines are now almost forgotten, although fortunes were made during their continuance.

In 1862, 1863, and 1864, the most thorough pro-specting was done through all the mountainous regions of the Territory, and many rich and valuable discov-eries were made at different points. Some of these discoveries were back of the Colorado River to the east of La Paz and Ehrenburg, but owing to a want of water have never been worked extensively. Could water be obtained for hydraulic washing, these local-ities would pay exceedingly well for many years. Dry washing machines have of late been introduced, which, under favorable circumstances, work quite sat-isfactorily, and it is supposed they will be so im-proved as to produce good results, and be the means of working out large tracts of placer mines, where it would be impossible to obtain a water supply. If perfectly successful they will add much to the product of the gold placers.

In 1862 and 1863, old Uncle Joe Walker, Paul Weaver, Jack Swilling, Henry Wickenburg, Mr. Peeples, and other noted prospectors and pioneers, devoted much time to the exploration of Central and Northern Arizona, and discovered many rich placers on the Hassayampa, Lynx, Big Bug, and other Creeks, in what is now Yavapai County, and in July, 1863, the rich placers of Weaver Gulch were discovered by them, and a Mexican working with Weaver, Swilling, Peeples, & Co. discovered Rich, or Antelope Hill, about the same time. This hill is twenty-eight miles north of Wickenburg, and near the road running from Wickenburg to Prescott. Weaver Gulch is on the east of the Rich Hill, and both the summit of the hill and the gulch were enormously rich. Antelope Hill was one of the most strange discoveries ever yet made in mining. The summit is some two thousand feet above the surrounding valleys below, and on it there is a slight depression, resembling a saddle back, of less than one acre of ground with but little earth covering the granite rock. In this depression of land a few men took out, in less than three months, $108,000 in nugget gold, from the size of a pin head to that of five or six hundred dollars in value.

A common belt or hunter's knife was the only implement used in the work, the gold being found in crevices and pockets, and to some extent on the smooth, bare rock. The gold was worn smooth and

round, like that found in the rivers and gulches of
California and elsewhere. How the gold came upon
the mountain's summit in such quantities, smooth and
water-worn, is a query which has puzzled most old
miners, who advocate different theories; but the most
natural explanation is, that a rich surface lode of
gold-bearing quartz, running across the mountains,
became decomposed and in the process of time, including perhaps many thousand years, the action of
water, and wearing away of the rocks by erosion, had
rounded and worn smooth the gold, and left it as
when discovered. Work is yet carried on at Weaver
Gulch, and on Antelope Hill, and some large nuggets
are occasionally found.

A half million dollars or more has been taken from
these mines, and when water is plenty in the gulch
fair wages can yet be made.

Another rich mining camp was at the " Placeritas,"
some fifteen miles northeast of Antelope Hill, where
large quantities of gold have been extracted, and
which are yet worked during the rainy seasons of the
year.

The mines on the Hassayampa Creek, ten miles
south of Prescott, have been worked since 1863, and
are yet yielding well in different localities.

The mines on Lynx Creek, ten miles east from
Prescott, have also been worked since 1863, and have
yielded large amounts of gold. They are yet worked

to some extent, as also the mines on Big Bug, Turkey, and other small creeks in Bradshaw Range, east and south of Prescott.

The " Cañada de Oro," thirty-five miles north from Tucson, in Pima County, is an extensive and rich placer gold deposit, and was worked a hundred years or more since by the Jesuits, who employed Indian laborers. Evidences of their work can yet be seen. The Cañada de Oro Creek furnishes water sufficient for hydraulic mining at these placers, and with the expenditure of a few thousand dollars a successful mining camp would spring into life at this locality. Some gentlemen in Tucson have located these mines, and it is to be hoped that they will soon push their work to a success.

In the winter of 1874–75, some rich placers were discovered in the northern spurs of the Santa Rita mountains, by Messrs. Smith, Ray, Hand, and others, which have yielded quite well, and which would yield a large amount of gold, was there water sufficient for hydraulic working. The yield has been remarkably large for the small amount of water that can be utilized for washing out the gold.

Many other placers have been discovered in different portions of the Territory, some of which are very rich but not extensive. The placer mines of Arizona are not extensive, like those of California in its early days, and perhaps the world will never see again the like, either in extent or richness, as **was** witnessed in California from 1849 to **1860.**

Wonderful reports have been circulated, **from** time to time, of rich placers **in** the northern and eastern parts of the Territory, which are said **to** have been seen **by** explorers long since, **or by** captives among the Apaches, and several expeditions have been fitted out for **their** discovery, but **as** yet **without** success. Some **of these** wonderful reports may be **true, but** doubtless many **of them are** more imaginary **than real.**

The great **and** permanent mineral wealth of the territory is in its **numerous rich and** extensive lodes of gold, silver, copper, and lead.

These lodes are found in almost every mountain, hill, and picacho peak in the Territory. Wherever one may **go,** north, south, east, or west, these lodes are found in **almost** endless **profusion.**

In Yuma County, in the southwestern part of the Territory, the most prominent mines are those of the Castle Dome district, forty miles northeast from Yuma. These **mines are** principally argentiferous galena and copper. The lodes are large and well defined, and most of them are very **rich.**

The principal argentiferous galena lodes are the Flora Temple, a four foot vein **owned** by N. Gunther & Co.; **the** Buckeye, a four **foot** vein owned by Miller, Berry, & Co.; the McLane, a four foot vein owned by Charles E. McLane; the Little Willie, a

two and a half foot vein, owned by William P. Miller
& Co.; the Big Dome, a three foot vein owned by E.
Battis, all of which yield from thirty to sixty-five per
cent. lead, and from twenty to thirty ounces of silver
per ton.   There are other lodes equally as promising
as the foregoing.

The principal copper lodes in the district are as
follows: The Montezuma, an enormous twelve foot
vein, owned by Messrs. Miller & Minear; the Cortez,
another great vein, twelve feet wide, owned by G. D.
Roberts & Co.; the Ellen Gowen, a seven foot vein
owned by William P. Miller; the St. Charles, a six
foot vein owned by Charles Baker & Co.   The two
first of these give a yield of thirty to sixty per cent.
of copper, and from thirty to forty-five ounces per ton
in silver.   The Ellen Gowen vein yields from thirty
to forty-five per cent. of copper, and over sixty ounces
of silver per ton.   The St. Charles vein yields about
the same as the others in copper, and in places is very
rich in silver, yielding at times over one hundred
ounces per ton.   Numerous other locations have been
made in the district, enough to warrant the belief,
that when this district is fully opened the yield of
silver, copper, and lead, will be very large, and add
much to the future product of the country.

The Castle Dome mines are in the Colorado River
range of mountains, and from ten to twenty miles
east of the river, and are easily approached from

Castle Dome Landing, where a brisk little town is being built up. Further north, in the same mountain range, there are locations of gold and silver mines at different points, for two hundred miles or more, some of which are very promising.

The Planet Copper Mine is in the extreme northern part of Yuma County, on the south of Bill Williams Fork, which stream is the dividing line between Yuma and Mohave counties. The mine is twelve miles east of Aubrey on the Colorado River, and was discovered in 1863, and has been worked in a desultory manner ever since. The ore yields from twenty-five to sixty per cent. in copper, and there has been a total yield of ore from the mine of over 8,000 tons, most of which has been shipped to, and sold in San Francisco at a fair profit.

The distance from Aubrey to San Francisco by water, being about 2,200 miles, and the freight high, it will be readily perceived that ore must be very rich to pay freight and other charges, and return a profit to the owners.

Mohave County is the northwestern one of the Territory, and a large portion of it is distinctly a mineral region. From Bill Williams Fork on the south, and extending thence north through the region of the Sandy, and thence through the Hualapai, Cerbat, Peacock, and other mountain ranges, there is a continued succession of mineral veins of great extent and richness. Many of these veins have been opened with the most flattering prospects, and some are being thoroughly worked. In the southern part of the county the lodes are very large, being from ten to nearly or quite one hundred feet wide, and traceable in some instances for many miles. In the central part of the county, in the northern spurs of the Hualapai Mountains, and in the Cerbat and Peacock mountains, the mineral lodes are not as large as further south, but extremely rich. The principal veins are argentiferous galena, yet there are many promising lodes of gold, and some almost wholly of silver. But few of the many hundreds and thousands of mines located in Mohave County can be specially mentioned, but sufficient to give the reader a general idea of the mineral wealth of the county.

The McCracken Mine is in the southern part of Mohave County, thirty miles east of the Colorado River, with a good roadway back and forth. It is six miles north of Bill Williams Fork, and twelve miles west of Sandy Creek. This mine was discovered August 17, 1874, by Messrs. McCracken and Owen, who yet own a large interest in the mine. It is now incorporated under the laws of California, with the Hon. Eugene Casserly as President, I. C. Bateman, Vice-president, and H. Augustus Whiting, Secretary.

The lode runs nearly due north and south, directly over a high mountain spur, known as McCracken

Hill. This hill has an elevation of about two thousand feet above the surrounding valleys. It is an
immense vein, being in places over eighty feet wide
at the surface. It is traceable for about two miles
by surface out-cropping, and out-crops at different
places on the south for ten or fifteen miles.

In some respects this mine differs from all others
on the Pacific Slope, the formation being a spar
gangue or matrix, in granitic or primitive formation.
Not a particle of quartz has been found in the mine,
and as quartz has ever been considered the true
matrix of gold and silver, the mine is a curiosity,
and well worth the study of the scientific. The out-
croppings of the mine on the summit of McCracken
Hill can be seen for many miles, the spar having a
dark burned appearance, caused by the hot burning
sun of thousands of years. At a distance it looks
like a black volcanic dyke, and for many years prospectors had so considered it, and had passed by the
mountain without an examination. The McCracken
Company own two mining claims of fifteen hundred
feet each in length, named the Senator and Alta.
The mine is now the best developed in the Territory,
having over seven hundred feet of shafting, and over
twelve hundred feet of tunnels. The deepest shaft
is three hundred and sixty-seven feet, and the shafts,
and over one thousand feet of the tunnels are in vein
matter all the way. The first class milling ore gives

by assay an average of $96 per ton, and the company's ten stamp mill at Greenwood, on the Sandy, works this ore up to sixty-five per cent. of the assay. The bullion produced averages 985 fine.

The second class milling ore, of which over five thousand tons are now on the dump pile, gives by assay over $65 per ton.

Twenty samples, taken promiscuously by the author from the dump pile, gave by assay $67.54 per ton. There are small stratas of carbonate ore carrying much lead, and excellent for smelting, which has sold in San Francisco for an average of $237 per ton, in silver, and yielding in addition twenty per cent. of lead. In the different shafts, tunnels, and drifts, the ore has in no place been worked out from hanging to foot walls, and therefore the actual width of vein matter at one, two, and three hundred feet depth, is unknown. In seven different chambers, the workings are from twenty-five to forty-two feet wide, and there is sufficient assurance to pronounce the McCracken one of the great mines of the world. In addition to the ten stamp mill at Greenwood, the company are now making arrangements to erect a new and much larger quartz mill the present year.

Cost of labor at the mine and mill four dollars per day. Wood, delivered, costs five dollars per cord. The cost of hauling ore from the mine to the mill is twelve dollars per ton. The amount of ore now mined, and working value, is, as near as can be ascertained, as follows: Two thousand tons of first class ore at sixty-five dollars per ton, working value, and five thousand tons of second class ore at forty-five dollars per ton, working value, gives a total of $355,000 of ore now mined. The great want at the mine at present is water, of which none has yet been developed in the mine, and for drinking, culinary, and other purposes, water is now brought from Castenado's well, eight miles distant.

The company's office is at rooms 7 and 9 Hayward's Block, San Francisco, where further and full information can be obtained of the mine, etc.

The first north extension of the McCracken is the San Francisco Mine, also incorporated, which is being opened successfully, and a large mill is to be erected the present year for working the ores, which are equally promising, both in extent and richness, to the McCracken. The extensions south are also being opened, and all look well.

Six miles south the vein out-crops again, and at this point Messrs. Cory and Potts, and some other parties, have good prospects for valuable and extensive mines.

The whole country to the north from the McCracken Mine, and from Greenwood for over one hundred miles, contains continued successions of mineral lodes of wondrous extent and richness. These mines are mostly argentiferous galena, some of them having a fair showing of gold. By a judicious expenditure of time and money, this whole extent of country will in due time become a source of great mineral wealth.

In the river range of mountains to the northwest of the McCracken Mine, there are numerous lodes of gold and silver, some of which have been worked in former years, but are now lying idle. Among the number is the Moss Gold Mine, from which much rich mineral was taken in years past. This mine is fifteen miles east from Camp Mohave, on the Colorado River.

In the northern portion of the Hualapai Mountains, there are many valuable mines of both gold and silver.

The Dean Mine, gold bearing, has been successfully opened with the most flattering prospects, sufficient to induce the company to erect a ten stamp mill, which will be erected the present year.

The American Flag Mine, silver bearing, owned by Mr. Shoulters, has been fully opened, and is very rich. Fifty tons of ore worked in the Mineral Park Mill, gave a product of from $300 to over $1,000 per ton in refined silver bullion. The American Flag Mine is near the summit of the Hualapai Mountains, and about thirty-five miles southeast from Mineral Park.

One hundred or more mines have been located in the Hualapais, but to the present time but few of them have been opened. Many of them give promise of exceeding richness, and the district, when well developed, will yield a large amount of gold and silver bullion. Wood and water are both abundant, offering fine inducements for both mining and milling operations.

The Cerbat Mountains, for an extent of thirty miles north and south, are a perfect network of mineral veins, including gold, silver, and lead, and of exceeding richness. The mineral lodes of the Cerbat range are small in comparison to those in the southern part of Mohave County, but make up to a great degree in richness what they lack in size and extent. These lodes range from one to three feet in width at a depth of twenty to one hundred feet. Many of them have been fully opened and prospected, and are now being worked successfully. The great hindrance to successful mining operations in the Cerbat Mountains, has been the want of reduction works. This has been partially remedied by the erection of a five stamp quartz mill at Mineral Park, which was put in successful operation February 22, 1876. The Mineral Park Mill Company have, since their mill was put in operation, worked ore for many different mines, all of which has paid extremely well, running from $100 to $1,000 per ton. A few only of the mines can be mentioned, of the hundreds in the Cerbat Mountains.

Cerbat, the county seat of the county, is in the southern spurs of the mountains, Stockton Hill being three miles northeast, and Mineral Park six miles to the north. This description of location will give the reader some idea of the particular locality of the mines hereafter mentioned.

The Fontenoy Mine, one mile east of Cerbat, is well opened by five shafts from twenty-five to one hundred feet each. The vein matter is eight inches to two feet wide, and works from $142 to $530 per ton in silver. Seventeen tons sold in San Francisco for over $500 per ton. Owners, Canavan & Mulligan.

The New York Mine, owned by Mulligan, is but a short distance from the Fontenoy and very similar to it. The ore pays from $100 to $600 per ton in silver.

The Sixty-three Mine, two miles northeast from Cerbat, was discovered in 1863, and has been successfully worked at intervals since that time. Over fifty tons of ore sold in San Francisco for $600 per ton, and large amounts of ore have been worked at the Mineral Park Mill and elsewhere, paying an average of $200 per ton in refined bullion. The vein matter is from one to three feet wide. The mine is incorporated, and the company are erecting reduction works at Cerbat, under the superintendence of Mr. Seale, one of the owners.

The Mocking-bird Mine, a half mile from the Sixty-three Mine, has a fine two foot vein of gray and blue sulphurets of silver, inclosing specimens of green horn silver. The ore assays from $200 to $1,000 per ton, and twenty tons worked in the Mineral Park Mill gave an average of $700 per ton, silver bullion. Owners, Riley & Co. successor to Miley & Riley, the original owners.

At Stockton Hill there are a large number of promising mines now opened and being worked. Among the number is a cluster of five, named respectively the Little Tiger, Dolly Varden, Cupel, Edward Everett, and Alba Stevens; all of which are quite rich in silver, and from eight to twenty inches of vein matter. Fifty tons of ore from these veins sold in San Francisco for over $500 per ton, and a large amount has been worked in the country. All has paid an average of over $200 per ton. Owners, Messrs. Cory & Potts.

There are many other lodes of silver running through this portion of the Cerbat Mountains, some of which have been opened and are now being worked to some extent. Among the number are the Tiger, Monitor, Franklin, I. X. L., Legal Tender, Snowflake, Lorena, Continental, Little Chief, etc., etc. All of the foregoing are rich veins from one to four feet wide, and the ore assays from $100 to $1,000 per ton. Selected specimens assay as high as $5,000 to $10,000 per ton. There is no doubt but Stockton Hill will ere long make a fine showing of her product of silver bullion. A quartz mill is much needed, and one for custom work would pay well, as fifty dollars per ton would be readily paid for reducing ores.

The Oro Plata Mine carries both gold and silver, as its name implies. It is two and a half miles north from Cerbat, a well defined two foot vein, owned by Messrs Cody and Layne, who have several other good mining properties in the Cerbat Range. The ore pays from $200 to $1,000 per ton. Large quantities have been worked in years past by Mexicans, in the common arastra, with large profits.

To the south and southwest of Cerbat are a large number of mines, mostly argentiferous galena, and gold intermixed with silver. Of the number the Vanderbilt, Champion, and Twins, owned by the Cerbat Mining Company, are among the most prominent. The Vanderbilt and Twins carry both gold and silver, and yield by working from $100 to $400 per ton. The Champion is a large six foot vein, carrying some free gold, with silver and lead, and works about $70 per ton.

The O'Fallon Mine, four miles south of Cerbat, is owned by Johnson & Co., and carries both gold and silver, — vein two feet wide. A shipment of several tons of ore to San Francisco paid the owners an average of $300 per ton.

There are many scores of other mines located around Cerbat, equally as promising as those mentioned. Those east of the town are mostly silver, while those to the west, running north and south, are gold and silver, and some heavy lodes of argentiferous galena.

At and around Mineral Park, in all directions, there are numerous rich and promising mines of silver and argentiferous galena, with a small percentage of gold in some, and an intermixture of other mineral substances. Some of these have been opened and are being worked quite successfully, among which are the following : —

The Keystone Mine, incorporated in California, is a few hundred yards north of the town, and has a vein of mineral from one to three feet in width, consisting of gray antimonial silver, carrying ruby and native silver, zinc pyrites and sulphurets of iron, and a trace of copper. Several hundred tons of this ore worked in the Mineral Park Mill has yielded an average of $200 per ton in refined bullion, and some lots have worked as high as $500 per ton. The claim west of the Keystone Mine, and on the same lode, is owned by the Hon. William H. Hardy & Co., and is equally promising.

The Lone Star Mine is one mile northeast of the town, and is incorporated under the laws of Arizona. It carries beautiful ore, rich in horn, ruby, and native silver, and yields in working from $200 to $600 per ton. The mine is well developed, and gives promise of becoming a splendid and permanent property.

The Metallic Accident Mine, discovered by accident as the name implies, is owned by T. J. Christie, its discoverer, who located it but little over one year since. The mining property covered by the Metallic location consists of a large and heavy lode of low grade ore on the surface, and includes several small veins or feeders, which run into the main lode. These feeders are extremely rich and are from eight to fourteen inches wide. Some thirty tons sold in San Francisco for $1,000 per ton. This was first class selected ore; specimens from this mine assay thousands of dollars per ton. Second class ore yields from $300 to $500 per ton. There is but little doubt that when this mine is worked to a proper depth, it will become one of the most productive in the Territory.

She-rum Peak is the highest point of the Cerbat Mountains, four miles northeast from Mineral Park, and well up its southern side there is an immense vein of low grade ore, located by Messrs. Mix & Co., which in time will become a great and valuable mining property.

The Index Mine, owned by Messrs. Haas & Co., is a good twenty inch vein, one mile northeast of Mineral Park, from which five tons of ore worked in the Mineral Park Mill yielded an average of $236 per ton in silver.

The Laporte Mine, owned by Davison & Co., south of the Index, gave by assay $534 per ton, and the ore will work from $200 to $400 per ton. A large number of other mines similar to the foregoing are well prospected, and some are being worked quite successfully.

Many heavy lodes of fine smelting ore are in the vicinity, which carry from twenty to sixty per cent. of lead, and from thirty dollars to one hundred dollars per ton in silver. L. C. Welbourne, and others, have locations of this character, some of which are to the west and southwest of town, and some to the west and north from She-rum Peak.

Chloride Flat is six miles north of Mineral Park, in the low foot hills and level land on the west of the Cerbat Range. This district was prospected and worked to some extent ten or twelve years since, but owing to the continued hostility of the Hualapai Indians, who murdered many of the miners, and from other causes, the camp became almost deserted, and remains so to the present time. Two smelting furnaces were at one time erected at Chloride, one of which is now in ruins, and the other has remained idle for several years. The ores of this district are mostly chlorides, and heavy veins of argentiferous galena. Some indications of cinnabar exist, but none sufficient to warrant the belief that that mineral exists there in paying quantities. One of the first locations made at Chloride Flat was on what is called Silver Hill, in 1864, but operations were broken up by the murder of those working it by the Hualapais, one being shot at the windlass, and two others killed by stones while in the shaft. Several other miners were killed in the vicinity about the same time, and for years all work was virtually broken up. The mine on Silver Hill is a four foot vein, and the ore pays from $100 to $300 per ton. No systematic work has been done on it for years, but just sufficient to keep up a title to the mine. This is the case with thousands of mines in the Territory, and though the law operates in some respects to the benefit of prospectors and miners, its general tendency is to retard the advancement and prosperity of the Territory. In the older States, during the past few years of hard times, thousands of landholders complain of being "land poor," and the same may be said of hundreds of miners who own locations in many different mining districts, and are unable to develop any of them, yet hold on to all, hoping, Micawber like, that something will turn up to their advantage. Could miners see, and understand, that one well developed mine is worth more than a hundred undeveloped ones, and that by continual prospecting and locating new mines, they are continually growing poorer and poorer, they and the country would both enter upon a new career of prosperity by the new departure. Miners and prospectors, think of this, and act for your own and the country's good. The following are some of the most conspicuous mines at Chloride Flat : —

The Schuylkill Mine is close by the old Baker furnace, a well defined four foot vein of fine argentiferous galena, and a good smelting ore. It yields from twenty to sixty per cent. lead, and an average of $45 per ton in silver.

The Schenectady Mine is a parallel lode to the Schuylkill, and to the east a few hundred yards. The ore is similar in character but richer in silver, yielding from $50 to $200 per ton.

The Albany Mine is the first extension north on the Schenectady Lode, and is equally promising. The vein widens out in places to eight feet, and yields some fine carbonate ore. The Schenectady and Albany mines have a solid body of mineral two feet wide, and the vein matter is fully four feet.

The Empire Mine is one mile further up the ravine, an immense lode, from two to twenty feet wide, of argentiferous galena and chloride ores, which yield an average of $210 to $256 per ton by actual working. Selected specimens assay $3,000 per ton. The mine is owned by the Cerbat Mining Company, of which W. H. Raymond of San Francisco is one of the principal stockholders. The company have many fine locations at Choride, and also at Cerbat.

To the west of the Empire Mine, some four hundred yards, Mr. Raymond has individually a mine called the Sunday-school, from which two lots of ore have been worked, one paying $191 per ton, and the other $500 per ton. Both of the last named mines are good milling ores.

The Blue Dick, Senator, and Hermit mines, are all less than one mile east from the Empire, and are owned respectively by Winham & Reany, Ashton, and Mr. Reany. They each carry silver, lead, and a trace of gold, and the owners claim a fine showing of cinnabar.

Independence Mine No. 1 is one mile east from Chloride Flat, a well defined six foot vein of argentiferous galena, yielding by assay from $50 to $500 per ton in silver.

Independence No. 2 is one mile northeast from Chloride, and is owned by Ridenour & Spear. The vein is three feet wide, and ten tons of the ore sold in San Francisco for $480 per ton.

The Oriental Mine, owned by E. Martin Smith, is south of Independence No. 1, and the vein matter, which is from five to twenty feet wide, assays from $100 to $300 per ton. The ore is a carbonate and argentiferous galena, with a trace of gold.

The Rose Bud and Porter mines are midway between Chloride and Mineral Park, having well defined veins of mineral. Ore from the Rose Bud paid by arastra working $300 per ton, and thirty tons from the Porter sold in San Francisco for $300 per ton. At a depth of fifty feet these veins run into a water formation and change from chlorides and carbonates to rich sulphurets.

The Black Snake Mine, in the same locality, is owned by W. M. Hardy. The ore is a fine chloride, which by mill process yields from $200 to $300 per ton.

The Conner Mine, one mile from the Black Snake, is a rich chloride and carbonate ore, with considerable gold. One lot of thirty tons yielded $400 per ton, and selected ore assays as much as $5,000 per ton. It is owned by Messrs. Canavan & Smith.

The Quaker Mine, a half mile north of Chloride Camp, is a large lode, varying from ten to twenty-two feet in width. It is a low grade ore, yielding from $30 to $60 per ton in silver. The ores are sulphurets, carbonates, and argentiferous galena.

The first extension north on the Quaker Lode is owned by Messrs. Towle & Co., and is called the Cady Mine, and is similar in character and extent to the Quaker.

The Virginia Mine, one mile northwest, is a good two foot vein of gray chloride and sulphurets of silver, which assay from $100 to $1,000 per ton. It is owned by H. Ashton.

The Pennsylvania Mine is owned by O. Groom, and

is a four foot vein of chloride ore, two miles west of
Chloride Camp. At a depth of forty feet, it changes
to rich sulphurets at the water line. Fine specimens
of horn silver are intermixed with the chloride ore.
Ten tons of this ore gave an average yield of $200
per ton, and selected ore assays $1,000 per ton.
When suitable hoisting and pumping works are
erected, and the mine worked thoroughly, it will become a valuable property.

The Diana Mine, owned by Rogers & Doniphan,
and the Pink Eye Mine, owned by J. Barnes & Co.,
are one half mile east from the Pennsylvania, and
each have veins of from two to four feet wide of rich
chloride ores, which assay from $300 to $3,000 per
ton. Thirty-five tons gave by working over $300
per ton average.

There are numerous other lodes of equally valuable mineral in and around Chloride Flat. Many
of these run well up in the foot hills of the Cerbat
Range, and others extend far down into the Sacramento Valley to the west.

In the main range of the mountains north of
She-rum Peak many locations have been made, but
few of them, however, have been thoroughly prospected or worked. The whole range is mineral bearing, except a narrow strip on its eastern declivity.
But few of the hundreds of mines located in the Cerbat Mountains have as yet been opened or worked,

but enough of them have been thoroughly prospected
to warrant the belief that these mountains have an
almost inexhaustible supply of the precious metals.

Prospecting is as brisk as ever, and new discoveries are being made continually. Wood is quite
plentiful in the mountains and in places there are
fine springs of water, yet there is a scarcity of water
at present for large reduction works. When the
mines are worked to sufficient depth, a good water
supply will be obtained for all practical purposes.
At Chloride Flat, and Stockton Hill, the water is
excellent for drinking and culinary purposes, but at
Mineral Park and Cerbat, much of the spring water
is strongly impregnated with mineral, and unpleasant
to strangers.

The Peacock Mountains are about twenty-five
miles east of the Cerbat Range, and to the east of
the beautiful Hualapai Valley, which intervenes between the two ranges. In the Peacock Mountains
some fine mineral lodes have been located, one of
which is deserving of a full and special mention. In
October, 1874, William Ridenour, S. Crozier, and two
others parties discovered a wonderful rich lode, which
they named the Hackberry Mine, in honor of a large
hackberry tree near a spring of the same name.
This tree gave them shelter and shade, and under
its protecting branches they made their home for
many weeks. Prior to the discovery of this mine,

the party had been on a prospecting tour to the
north, far down towards the Grand Cañons of the
main and little Colorado, where they were attacked
by Indians and barely escaped with their lives, losing,
however, their animals, mining tools, food, and clothing.   After long wandering, they succeeded in reaching Mineral Park, nearly dead with fatigue and
hunger.   After a few days of rest, they again started
out on another prospecting tour, and were fortunate
in finding the Hackberry Mine, which is destined to
become one of the noted ones of our country.

The Hackberry Mine is in the foot hills of the
eastern declivities of the Peacock Mountains.   The
lode has a nearly due north and south course, and
has been traced for several miles.   Two locations
were made by the discoverers, the Hackberry and
the Hackberry South.   Messrs. Ridenour & Crozier,
in the division, took the Hackberry, and the other
partners the Hackberry South, which they sold soon
after to the Mineral Park Mill Company for $12,000.
Messrs. Ridenour & Crozier, though without money,
had what is better, grit, vim, and energy, and a good
mining experience, and went to work with a will to
develop the mine. In the winter of 1875–76, Messrs.
Davis & Randall erected a five stamp mill near the
Hackberry spring, and when completed in March,
1876, it was included in the Hackberry property, and
Messrs. Davis & Randall became part owners in the

property. In October, 1876, the property was incorporated at San Francisco, under the laws of California, with William H. Raymond as President, and E. Martin Smith, Secretary, the character of both these gentlemen being such as to give perfect confidence in the organization, and in the value of the property.

The Hackberry Mine has been opened at five different points to a depth of fifty to over two hundred feet, and all the openings show a continuous body of rich mineral, from one to five feet wide, which increases in width regularly as the work goes down. On the surface the pay ore is from one foot to sixteen inches wide, and at two hundred feet deep the ore has widened out to five feet, and equally rich as at the surface. The ore body is all worked in the mill, and pays regularly $200 per ton.

Rich stratas are found which will yield $1,000 to the ton. To a depth of one hundred and sixty feet the ore is a free milling ore, and does not require roasting; but below that depth rich sulphurets abound, and it requires roasting. The company are now erecting a furnace, and when completed the product of silver bullion will be much increased. Over five hundred tons of ore have been worked, with results as before stated.

The geological formation is granite, with dykes of slate, quartzites, talc, and pipe clay. The inclosing granite walls are from thirty to one hundred feet

apart. The ore at the mill battery has averaged
$247 per ton, and there is now mined nearly one
thousand tons of ore ready for working when the furnace is completed and in operation. Adjoining the
wall rock of granite on the east is a quartzite from
five to fifteen feet wide, then a talc of about the
same width, then the mineral vein ; to the west of
the mineral body a pipe and fire clay fifteen to thirty
feet, then a narrow, soft quartzite, and adjoining this
a red water-bearing conglomerate, which meets the
granite wall-rock on the west. A careful and critical
examination conveys the impression that at a sufficient depth the whole space between the granite
walls will be filled with mineral, in which event it
will become a Bonanza mine, equal to the most
noted in the world.

When incorporated, Messrs. Ridenour and Crozier
owned three fourths of the mine and mill, and Messrs.
Davis and Randall one fourth. The foregoing is but
a brief and imperfect description of the Hackberry
Mine, made from a personal examination by the
author. $75,000 of bullion produced to date.

To the east and north of the Hackberry Mine
are other promising mining locations worthy of mention, but which cannot be described or enumerated
in this work.

Wood of an excellent quality and in abundance exists in the Peacock Mountains, close by the Hack-

berry Mill and Mine, and many fine springs of excellent water.

The eastern part of Mohave, and the western part of Yavapai County, are to a certain extent destitute of mineral, yet in several localities good indications exist, and when the country is thoroughly prospected, no doubt valuable discoveries will be made.

The central and southern portions of Yavapai County, which is the northeastern county in the Territory, may be said to be literally a mass of mineral lodes of gold, silver, copper, and lead, and a volume might be written descriptive of them without exhausting the subject. Silver, gold, and lead are found over the whole extent, and copper principally in the mountains and foot hills twenty to thirty miles southwest of Prescott, and on the upper waters of the Santa Maria Creek, which is the main eastern branch of Bill Williams Fork.

From the southern spurs of the Bradshaw Mountains, near Salt River, and extending thence north for a hundred miles or more, to the northern spurs of the Black Hills, there is a continued succession of rich lodes of gold, silver, and argentiferous galena.

In the northern and western portions of this great mineral belt, gold predominates, and in the central and southern, silver; but the two minerals are found intermixed to some extent through the whole belt.

Some good locations of copper are also found in the
eastern declivities and foot hills of the Bradshaw
and contiguous mountains. Twenty miles southeast
from Prescott, and thirty miles northeast, in and
around the Black Hills, many fine veins of copper
have been located, but they will not be worked much
until the country is traversed by railroads.

The following is a brief description of some of the
principal mines in Yavapai County : —

The Vulture Mine is in the southwest part of the
county, some ten miles south from Wickenburg, and
was discovered in October, 1863, by Henry Wickenburg, one of the early prospectors of the Territory.
It is gold bearing, and a rich and extensive lode.
Mr. Wickenburg worked it for some time alone, and
then James A. Moore became interested with him.
It required great nerve and energy to work it, as the
Indians were very hostile, requiring constant watch-
fulness and continued preparation for battle with
them. The mine was afterwards sold to the Vulture
Mining Company for $85,000, and was worked suc-
cessfully for a time, and yielded large amounts of
gold bullion, aggregating, as is believed, from one
to two million dollars. For reasons unknown to the
community, and under suspicious circumstances, work
both at the mill and mine was suddenly suspended,
and for several years the mill has lain idle. Some
three years since Mr. William Smith, who has re-

located a portion or all of the lode, erected a ten
stamp mill twelve miles to the east of the mine, on
the Hassayampa, and has been working the ore with
fair profit.

The vein is from two to twenty feet wide, and in
places of great richness. Mr. Smith has been working surface ore principally, which yields an average
of $35 per ton. Doctor Jones, one of the best in-
formed scientific miners in the Territory, is connected in some manner with Mr. Smith in the Vulture Mine, and has great confidence in its future.
The Doctor has many mining interests scattered far
and wide through the Territory, and is probably as
well informed respecting its mineral wealth as any
one there.

Many other lodes of gold and silver are located all
through the section of country in and about Wickenburg. Argentiferous galena lodes are also numerous, and one owned by a well-known old pioneer,
known as Black Jack, a few miles east of the Vulture Mine, is claimed to be one of the best for smelting purposes of any in the Territory.

In the mountains east of the Hassayampa Creek
several promising lodes have lately been discovered,
and are now being prospected with promises of good
results.

Further up the Hassayampa, in the vicinity of
Walnut Grove, and some twenty-five miles south

from Prescott, there are a number of rich mines of gold, and argentiferous galena, now being opened and worked. Messrs. A. Cullumber and son, Fred. Henry, and others, have exceedingly good prospects, and the Pinal Silver Mining Company have also some good locations, and have lately completed a smelting furnace of thirty tons daily capacity, which if successful will add much to the prosperity of the district. The company own the Crescent Mine among other mining properties, which is a well defined two foot lode of argentiferous galena, excellent for smelting, and which yields from twenty to forty-five per cent. lead, and from $20 to $100 per ton of silver. Selected ore yields much more in silver.

The company employ from twenty to forty men at the furnace and mine. C. D. Morrison, the Superintendent, is an old and experienced miner and smelter, and has great confidence in the success of the company.

The new discoveries of Cullumber, Henry, and others, are a few miles west of Walnut Grove, and some of them are wonderfully rich in gold.

Mr. Bowers, sheriff of Yavapai County, has a good gold mine in the same section of country, which has been worked to some extent.

Twenty miles east from Walnut Grove, in the Bradshaw Mountains, and about forty miles south

from Prescott, is the old Tiger Mine, discovered by
D. C. Moreland some years since, and opened and
worked to some extent.

The Tiger Lode is well defined with good wall
rocks, and from four to forty feet wide on the surface,
and has been traced and located a distance of over
two miles. The locators are mostly residents of the
Territory, are honest, but unfortunately most of them
are poor, and consequently unable to erect suitable
machinery to work the mine, or to treat the ores, and
the result is, this valuable mining property with its
untold millions of wealth has lain idle for years, and
must continue so for years to come, unless capitalists
shall take hold of the property and assist in the development of its long stored up wealth.

Two shafts have been sunk on the Tiger Mine to a
depth of one hundred feet, connected by a tunnel two
hundred and sixty feet long. There are several hundred tons of ore on the dump pile, taken out some
years since, which will work from $100 to $300 per
ton. Selected ore has been taken out which assays
as much as $7,000 per ton in silver.

The first extension south, owned by Messrs. Riggs,
Hammond, & Co., is now being opened, and looks
equally as promising as the original discovery. Several openings on the northern extensions also give
promise of grand results when thoroughly opened
and worked.

Whenever reduction works are erected for working
the rich ore of the Tiger Lode, a large and prosperous
mining town will spring into existence as if by magic,
and hundreds of thousands of dollars be added to the
productive wealth of the Territory.

To the north of the Tiger Mine, in a depression of
the mountains three miles distant, and known as the
Bradshaw Basin, are a large number of promising
mines of both gold and silver. Several of the gold-
bearing lodes are being worked continuously, and
the ore, worked by arastra process, pays from $60
to $120 per ton. Messrs. Luke, Collier, & Roach
own several fine mines, and Mr. Luke, who is an
active, wide-awake man, and ex-mayor of Prescott,
has made arrangements to erect suitable reduction
works the present season, which will add much to
the prosperity of the district.

Messrs. Luke & Co. own the Gretna and Idlewild mines, both of which are four foot veins, and
which have paid by actual working $464 per ton in
silver.

They also own the Thurman Mine, gold bearing,
a two and a half foot vein of solid sulphurets; also
some others nearly as promising. The ore from the
Thurman Mine yields from $40 to $200 per ton.

North of Bradshaw Basin, two miles, is the Del
Pasco Mine, a rich gold bearing lode, which has
been worked to some extent, but is now idle for
want of capital to erect reduction works.

To the east of the Del Pasco is the War Eagle Mine of Jackson Brothers & Co., about midway between the Tiger on the south and the Peck Mine on the north, and supposed by many to be the same lode. The War Eagle is a five foot vein, and has been worked to quite an extent. One thousand tons of the ore yielded from $60 to $500 per ton in gold and silver, the average being $50 in gold and $70 in silver, — a total average of $120 per ton.

Two miles north of the Jackson Mine is War Eagle Mine No. 2, on the same lode, now owned by Linn, Coe, & Co., who purchased it a few months since of Messrs. Goodwin & McKinnon, the original owners.

Before selling, Messrs. Goodwin & McKinnon took out and worked by arastra process several hundred tons of ore which paid them from $40 to $200 per ton, gold. The present owners are prosecuting work on the mine successfully, and at eighty feet depth are working a solid two foot vein which assays, in gold, from $50 to $1,200 per ton; and, in silver, from $25 to $50 per ton.

The Peck Mine, two miles north of the last named, is truly one of the great mines of the world. It is in the eastern declivities of the Bradshaw Mountains, and thirty miles east of south from Prescott.

The Peck was discovered and located June 17, 1875, by Messrs. Peck, Bean, Alexander, Jewell, and Cole, most of whom retain their interests in it. The mine has lately been incorporated under the laws of the Territory, with a capital of one million dollars, divided into one hundred thousand shares of ten dollars each. President, Hon. C. C. Bean; Secretary and Assayer, F. W. Blake: Office, Prescott, A. T.

When this mine was located its fortunate discoverers were, in mining phraseology, " down to bed rock," in other words, out of funds; but by untiring energy, and continuous work and management, assisted by a few noble hearted friends, the Peck Company are now on the road to wealth. A ten stamp quartz mill, the Aztlan, located six miles south from Prescott, has been purchased and paid for, the mine has been opened to a depth of two hundred and fifty feet, and a large amount of ore taken out and worked very successfully both by mill and furnace process.

The geological character of the country both east and west, a half mile from the mine, is granite, but between the granite formation, for a half mile to one mile in width, are numerous dykes of quartzites, slate, and porphyry, intermixed with granite, forming a splendid gangue for a rich and extensive mineral deposit. At a depth of two hundred and thirty feet the ore body is five feet wide, carrying a wonderful strata of almost solid chloride of silver, from eight to fourteen inches wide, which yields from $1,000 to $3,000 per ton in refined silver bullion. Selected ore assays from $10,000 to $26,000 per ton. First class ore has paid, **both** by mill and **furnace process, from** $1,000 to $1,600 per ton. Second **class ore** has paid, **by the** same process, an average of **over $400 per** ton.

The ore **from this mine is** transported by pack trains over twenty miles **to their mill, which** is quite expensive. **At a depth of 170 feet,** water enters the **mine, and it is expected that** at **not much** greater depth **a flow of water will be obtained sufficient** to **operate a ten** stamp mill, **in which event thousands** of **tons** of ore, which will yield **from $100 to $300 per** ton, can be worked at the mine, but which **will not** warrant the company in paying the great expense **of** packing to their present mill. The Aztlan Mill **is** now turning out some $10,000 of refined bullion **per week, and but** five **stamps are used, the** other five being **employed in working gold ores** for different parties.

The probable **future product of silver bullion from** the Peck Mine is **almost limitless. It is not the only** one in the district **however, as** there **are many other** locations which give promise of becoming its rivals, both in extent and richness.

The Silver Prince Mine, discovered some **time** subsequent to the discovery of the Peck, is a short **mile** southeast from the Peck, and is owned by its discoverers and locators, Messrs. Houghteling & Curtin. Both of these lodes have a north and south trend, and are parallel to each other.

Messrs. Houghteling & Curtin have accomplished wonders in opening and developing their mine, which is now in good condition for successful work, and have good buildings, work shops, assay office, etc., all in perfect order.

The ore from the Silver Prince Mine is quite similar to that of the Peck. Several tons of first class selected ore sold in San Francisco for $2,470 per ton, and second class ore for $818 per ton. Selected specimens assay as high as $14,000 per ton. The future of the Silver Prince is most promising.

The Black Warrior Mine, the first south extension of the Silver Prince, owned by Messrs. Smith, Buttrick, & Co., is very promising, and has been well prospected.

Several tons of ore from this mine sold in San Francisco for $1,200 per ton. This mine carries in places heavy bodies of rich argentiferous galena.

One mile north from the Peck Mine, and evidently on or quite near the Peck extension north, is a heavy out-cropping of copper, eight hundred feet in length, with a width of vein matter six to ten feet wide, which gives by assay from thirty to sixty per cent. copper. The location was discovered and is owned by Messrs. Roberts, Poland, & Boggs.

One mile northeast from the Peck Mine, there is an immense lode of low grade ore called the Wallace Mine, which is owned by some members of the Peck

Company. The vein matter is in some places eighty feet in width. At one point, there is a thin strata of salts of silver. This location will not pay to work now, but the time will come when the country is opened by railroads, when it will be a valuable property.

Scores of other valuable locations are within a short distance of the Peck and Silver Prince mines, many of which are being developed, among which is one owned by General A. V. Kautz, Military Commandant of the Territory.

On the route from the Peck Mine to Prescott, a distance of thirty miles, there is a continued succession of mineral veins of both gold and silver.

Some of them on the head waters of Turkey Creek have been well opened and are being successfully worked.

Wm. M. Buffum, Esq., has a quartz mill at that point, called the Crook Mill, which is in successful operation. It is run on gold ores exclusively, there being many rich lodes in the vicinity.

On the Hassayampa Creek, ten miles south of east from Prescott, S. O. Fredericks has a ten stamp mill with all the latest improvements in successful operation, working ore from his mine, the Senator Lode, which is one mile up the mountain to the south.

The Senator Mine is gold bearing, carrying a fair percentage of silver. The ore is a beautiful body of

sulphurets, the vein being five feet wide with vertical wall rocks of slate and granite. The whole of
the five foot ore body is worked, there being no assorting of mineral or refuse low grade ore. The
whole body of ore assays $85 dollars per ton in gold.
Until quite recently Mr. Fredericks has made no
effort to save the silver, and beside has lost a large
amount of the gold carried off in the undecomposed
sulphurets. With improved machinery, now in operation, a very large saving will be made over former
working, which however has been very profitable.
The Senator Mine has been worked to a depth of
two hundred feet, and a more regular body of ore of
uniform width and richness was never discovered.
In the whole depth of two hundred feet, and in all
the drifts, stopes, and tunnels, the width of the vein
will vary but a few inches from five feet. It is a
most valuable property, and in good hands.

Some three miles south of the Fredericks Mill, in
the southern declivity of the Hassayampa Mountains,
are several large and rich lodes of argentiferous galena, and other ores, one of which, the Davis Mine,
has been partially opened. The vein is fully fifteen
feet wide, and some selected ore, shipped to San
Francisco a few years since by the Hon. C. C. Bean,
was sold for several hundred dollars per ton. At
present these mines are difficult of access, as the
mountain spurs south of the Hassayampa Creek are

high and precipitous. There is no doubt but in a few years, some of the mines in this locality will be among the best in the Territory.

Between the Hassayampa and Prescott, there are many promising lodes, mostly of gold, some of which are now being opened and worked. Judge Brooks of Prescott has some good locations, as well as many other parties, and all have great hopes of realizing fortunes from their mines.

To the west of Prescott, from five to twenty miles, there is a gold bearing formation of considerable extent now being developed. Among those engaged in the work is Alexander Majors, Esq., one of the best known men west of the Mississippi River, and one respected by all men. In his old age he has settled down here to retrieve his fortunes, after having lost his all during the great civil war. Good wishes attend him from all, and a decided success would be hailed with delight by a host of sincere and earnest friends. The mine now being worked by Mr. Majors has a body of ore two feet wide, which assays from $40 to $200 per ton.

To the east of Prescott, from five to fifteen miles in width, and extending a long distance north and south, is a district of country literally filled with lodes of gold and silver, some of which are of remarkable richness. These mines are mostly in the mountains bordering on Lynx, Big Bug, and other creeks, where for many years placer and gulch gold mining has been carried on with success. Excellent water and timber abound in this district, which is of great advantage to mining operations.

The following are a few of the many mines in this section of country:—

The Accidental, a mine discovered in 1864, and at times worked more or less since that time, is a well defined vein of gold bearing quartz, from two to three feet wide, now owned by Messrs. Rice, Elliot Bros., & Co. The owners have twenty-two hundred feet in length on the lode, and the workings include two tunnels, one of two hundred and ninety feet in length, and one of one hundred and seventy feet. Shafts have also been sunk to a depth of one hundred feet. Both the tunnels and the several shafts are all in the pay ore. Over one thousand tons of ore have been worked, and it has paid from $30 to $80 per ton in gold. The company have a mill one mile below the mine, on Lynx Creek, where they have a thirty-five horse-power steam engine, with which they run four arastras day and night, and a thunderbolt quartz crusher. They work an average of six tons daily, working sixteen men at the mill and mine, paying an average of three dollars per day and board. The mine in places carries a heavy and rich body of silver ore, but as yet it has never been worked but for gold. The argentiferous galena ore found in the mine gives thirty per cent. in lead, and an assay value of $30 per ton in silver. The mine is well up in the mountains on the east side of Lynx Creek. So numerous are the mineral lodes in this district, one can count nearly one hundred from the summit of the mountain above the Accidental Mine. Some of them have been thoroughly prospected and give promise of exceeding richness.

Across the summit of the mountain to the east, on the head waters of Big Bug Creek, Messrs. Poland, Roberts, and others have some excellent mining property, both gold and silver. Among those owned by Poland & Roberts are the Poland, Belle, Bullion, Mesa, Turkey, and Bulger, all of which are good mines.

The Poland Mine is rich in both gold and silver, and the ore works from $122 to $310 per ton. There are heavy bodies of beautiful sulphate of lead in this mine. The Mesa and Turkey mines are both gold bearing, and both pay from $60 to $200 per ton. The others carry gold, silver, and lead.

In the Poland Mine are many beautiful specimens of white crystallized sulphate of lead, a rare mineral in all mining countries.

Passing down Big Bug Creek to the east, one meets at short intervals rich out-croppings of mineral, of both gold and silver. The Hon. C. E. Hitchcock and family, who live near the creek, some four miles

below the mountain **summit**, have several promising
locations, among which are the **Big Bug, Gen. Kautz,
Belle, Sunset, Sunrise, Twilight**, etc. **Some of them**
are rich in gold, **some in silver, and some are of argentiferous galena. Some years since, Mr.** Hitchcock
carried on at Big Bug successful mining operations,
but **during his absence** east on business, operations,
owing to mismanagement, entirely ceased, and like all
others of like character, debts accumulated, and mines
and machinery became involved **in** litigation, and an
entire loss of all invested became the inevitable **result.**

Excellent **water and good pine timber abounds in
the mountains along the Big Bug as well as upon
Lynx Creek.** Wherever **wood and water are** both
abundant the value of mining property is much en-
hanced.

From two to six miles north of Big Bug Creek, in
the eastern **foot** hills of the mountains, there are several very fine lodes **of** argentiferous galena ores,
which are fine **for** smelting, and **of the highest** grade.

The Silver Belt Lode **is one of the** best in the
country, and has yielded **a large amount of** bullion.
It is **a heavy two** foot **vein, and is now** being worked
on a lease **by Mr. Thompson, and the** ore is smelted
in the Agua **Frio Furnace,** a few miles distant. The
ore yields **a return of $300** per ton in silver, and
some over **twenty per cent. lead.**

The Kit Carson and Silver Flake mines are both of the same kind and character as the Silver Belt, and both are being successfully worked. The ores from these two mines yield from $100 to $600 per ton. The veins are from two to four feet wide, with well defined wall rocks.

During the past few months the three last named mines have produced several thousand pounds of bullion, the ore being worked in the Agua Frio Furnace, by Messrs Perkins & Shafer.

The Salvador Mine is a gold lode, three miles east from Prescott, with a good showing of silver. Ninety tons of the ore worked in the Aztlan Quartz Mill gave a total yield of over $7,000. The ore was worked by Messrs. Bowers & Richards. Work is progressing on this mine successfully.

To the northeast from Prescott for a distance of fifty miles through the Black Hills, and to the west of Camp Verde, there have been many mines of gold, silver, and copper, located during the past year, which from surface indications, indicate the existence of vast bodies of rich mineral. Some of these locations have been prospected to considerable extent, sufficient to warrant the belief that they are permanent true fissure veins.

The extreme northern and northeastern parts of the county of Yavapai have not been prospected to any extent, though the well known prospectors and explorers, Charley Spencer, Dan O'Leary, and some others, have made several expeditions into that portion of the Territory in search of some fabulous rich silver mines, which tradition asserts, were long since worked by the old Jesuit priests from California, a century or more since. These daring prospectors and Indian fighters have penetrated far down into the great cañons of the north, and relate wonderful stories of what they there discovered : of isolated bands of Indians living far down in the deep gorges and cañons of that region, where no white man's foot had ever trod, and where none can enter except by the descent from point to point of perpendicular wall rocks, hundreds and thousands of feet deep; of peach orchards, corn and pumpkin fields, almost hidden from view, down in the cañons near the rivers whose presence was heretofore unknown ; of masses of mineral running through the granitic formation of the cañon's sides, and of a thousand other interesting sights witnessed by them. Many other traditions exist respecting that great northern, and almost unknown country, of the finding many years since of rich gulches and ravines, where nuggets of gold could be picked up by the handful, of golden Indian bullets found after straggling Indian fights, of large masses of gold seen in the possession of Indians from time to time, and of many other wonderful stories hard to be believed. If any or all of such reports and traditions are true, they will in time be verified, for the impulse to search for gold is so strong in man that some of the hundreds of brave and reckless prospectors of the Territory will in the course of time find the localities indicated, at whatever cost and peril.

In the great Tonto Basin, a hundred miles east from Prescott, there are known to be rich placer mines, also wonderful lodes of gold and silver, but the basin has ever been the resort of all the Apache bands, and of the refugees who from time to time leave the Indian reservations for mischief and plunder, and consequently but few whites have been bold and reckless enough to explore and prospect that region of country, as most parts of the Territory have been explored and prospected. The march of the white man will no longer be stayed, and soon this almost terra incognita will be made to disburse freely from its long hidden stores of mineral wealth.

To the north of Camp Apache there is quite an extent of country having a sandstone formation, with limestone intermixed, in which have been found stratas of excellent coal, but they are so far from the white settlements, and from any market, no inducements have existed sufficient to cause them to be developed. With the construction of the Thirty-fifth Parallel Railroad, this coal formation will become a necessity, and a source of wealth and prosperity to the country.

But two other mineral belts remain to be described in Yavapai County, which are the new mines lately discovered by **Jack** Swilling, Jack Moore, **Bob Groom,** and others, **in the** southern **spurs** of the Bradshaw Mountains, west of the Black Cañon, and the **wonderful Clifton** Copper Mines in the **far** southeastern part of the county, near the **bound**ary line between Arizona and New Mexico.

The Black Cañon Mines were discovered but **a few** months since, and are of that wonderful rich character, characteristic of the Peck, Silver Prince, **and** others **previously mentioned.** They are about sixty miles south from Prescott, and ten miles west from the Black Cañon of Turkey Creek.

Within a **radius of five miles, a large** number of miners are now **at work** developing many lodes of rich silver ore, which yields from **$300** to $600 per ton.

Among the principal lodes opened and now being successfully worked are the Tip Top, Rescue, Silver Jack, Fourth of July, Nevada, McDerwin, **Fawn,** George, Swilling, and several **others equally prom**ising.

The Swilling **Mine, owned by Jack** Swilling, **has a four** foot vein carrying **a ten inch** strata of solid chloride ore. Ten tons paid in working, $513 **per** ton. Second class **ore** assays from **$100** to $300 per ton. The vein is well defined with good wall rocks.

The Tip Top Mine is owned by Jack Moore & Co., and is the best developed of any in the district. It has been thoroughly prospected by both shafts and tunnels. The vein is from fifteen inches to over two feet wide, and the ore assays from three hundred to thousands of dollars per ton. The ore worked has yielded an average of $550 per ton.

One mile up the cañon from the Tip Top Mine is a location owned by Messrs. Brunson & Barnum, who have a two foot vein from which they have mined several tons of ore worth over $500 per ton.

The Fawn Mine is on the Swilling Lode, and is owned by Mr. Mullen, who has a two foot vein of ore equally as rich as the others mentioned.

The George Mine shows rich ore at four different openings.

Two miles distant from the George Mine, Mr. J. Foy has taken out some very rich ore, which gave by assay $1,900 per ton.

D. C. Moreland, the original discoverer of the noted Vulture Mine, has also a good claim here, from which he is taking out quantities of $500 ore.

Bob Groom and other parties have locations quite similar, and equally as good as the foregoing. The ore from the Black Cañon Mines has to be freighted either to the Aztlan Mill, a distance by wagon road of seventy-five miles, or to the Smiths Mill south of

Wickenburg, a distance of over one hundred miles, at great cost and expense.

Good springs of water abound in and around this mining camp, but wood is scarce. When reduction works are erected conveniently near, and roads constructed, this new mining district will become one of the most prosperous in the Territory. Too high an estimate cannot be made of the vast amount of mineral wealth here stored up for man's use. The ores are easily worked, both by mill and furnace process, they being free carbonates and chlorides, with fine specimens of ruby and horn silver, in considerable quantities.

The wonderful Clifton Copper Mines were discovered several years since, and have been worked by different parties with eminent success. Among the leading operators are Messrs. Lazinsky and the Bennett Brothers, all of Silver City, New Mexico.

The ore is in vast bodies, virtually mountains of copper, and very pure, ranging from thirty to eighty-five per cent. Thousands of tons of copper have been worked by furnaces, of which there are a number in continual operation. There are from two hundred to four hundred men employed all the time at three to four dollars per day. These mines are about eighty miles west from Silver City, New Mexico, one hundred and seventy-five northeast from Tucson, and two hundred south of east from Prescott.

Of nearly eight thousand mining claims located and recorded in Yavapai County, the author has selected and described but a few as a type of them all, hoping to give to the public correct and reliable information respecting the great mineral wealth of the county, from which the reader can form a definite idea of its future mineral product, when all these thousands of mines, already located, shall be worked, together with thousands of others which are now undiscovered.

It should be borne in mind that nearly all the mines opened and worked in Yavapai County, and elsewhere in the Territory, have been located by men without money to operate with, relying entirely on muscle, energy, and perseverance, and that consequently the development of the mines has been slow and gradual.

The continued hostility of the Apache tribes has also been a serious hindrance to mining, as well as to all other industries in the Territory, and until two years past no man was safe from their murderous attacks in any part of the Territory. When we consider the isolated condition of the country, far from any great centres of civilization, remote from railroads, destitute of cheap and rapid transit, the wonder is, that so much has been done in the development of the Territory as has been accomplished to the present time.

8

Too much honor and praise cannot be given the
early pioneers of Arizona, who have, under all the
surrounding difficulties which have continually beset
them, continued their exertions towards developing
the Territory of Arizona — *the coming country of our
continent.*

Mining capitalists from abroad, both on the Pacific
and Atlantic slopes, are turning their attention to
Arizona, being fully convinced by what has been
already developed by hard labor alone, without any
considerable assistance from capitalists, that it is the
great mineral country of the world.

In this connection it is proper to remark, that several noble-hearted business men of Prescott have at
times assisted miners in the development of their
mines, without which assistance much delay and suffering would have ensued. Prominent among these
are the firms of C. P. Head & Co., Bowers & Richards,
L. Bashford & Co., William M. Buffum, John G.
Campbell, and others, to whom Yavapai County
owes much for its present prosperous condition.

Maricopa County is to the south of Yavapai, and
is distinctively more of an agricultural region than a
mining country. It is the great agricultural county
of the Territory, and as such has been fully described
in the chapter devoted to agriculture and farming.

The northern and eastern portion of Maricopa
County is a mining country, in which some good

mines have been located, and in the southeastern part is a portion of the newly-discovered and wonderfully rich Globe mining district, a district probably without a parallel. The main part of the district being in Pinal County, a brief description will be given of it in the description of the mines of that county.

Pinal County is south of Maricopa, and between Maricopa and Pima counties. The whole eastern portion of Pinal County is a mining country of exceeding richness. Good mines exist also in the western part of the county. No thorough prospecting was ever done through the Pinal, Apache, or Mazatzal Mountains, until 1875. The Globe Copper Mine, a mountain of copper, had been discovered, but nothing had been done to develop it. In the summer and fall of 1875 attention was attracted to the Pinal Mountains, and some gold placers were found sufficient to attract the attention of miners, who are ever on the alert to go in search of new diggings. The result was the discovery of wonderfully rich lodes of silver ore of almost fabulous extent, which are drawing to the district large numbers of miners and prospectors, as well as capitalists. During the past year, 1876, hundreds have flocked to this new El Dorado, and are opening the scores of rich mines already located. A brisk mining town has sprung into existence; quartz mills and furnaces are being erected, and the prospects are growing brighter and brighter, day by day, for this becoming one of the most prosperous mining camps on the continent.

This mining district is about twenty miles in length and twelve in width, and within this area about fifty distinct and well defined lodes of silver have been discovered, some of which are also rich in gold. The mineral lodes are from two to ten feet wide, and some of miles in length. The Globe Copper Mine is of enormous extent and exceedingly rich, and will yield from forty to eighty per cent. of refined copper.

One of the peculiarities of the Globe district is the wonderful plants of silver, — planchas de plata, — which are masses of almost pure silver nuggets, from a few pounds in weight to five hundred or more pounds. These nuggets are found in various localities, but more especially in and around Richmond Flat, where mining claims are staked off and dug up with pick and shovel like gold placers.

There is some mystery connected with these planchas de plata, many believing that they were thrown up from the depths below by volcanic action, but the more reasonable opinion prevails, that they are masses broken from the surface of the rich lodes during past ages, and have been washed and worn down to their present form and locality.

In connection with these planchas de plata, it may

be proper to mention another locality in Northern Sonora, and but a few miles south of the Arizona line, where in the past century some wonderful planchas of pure silver were found, one of which weighed twenty-nine hundred pounds, the record of it being yet kept at the port of Guaymas, on the Gulf of California.

The planchas of the Globe district have yielded many thousand dollars, one gentleman having secured and sold over $10,000 in value of his own discovery.

A few of the mines in the Globe district will be mentioned, being a fair average sample of the hundreds located.

The Rescue Mine has a three foot vein of silver ore which assays from $300 to $15,000 per ton. The lode is well defined, and well opened.

The Blue Cap Mine is a large and well defined vein, over three feet wide, and the ore assays from $500 to $5,000 per ton in silver. Horn and native silver is very abundant in the ore, as well as in many other lodes in the district.

The Helen Mine carries chloride, nugget, and horn silver, and the ore assays as high as $8,000 per ton. The vein is three feet wide and well defined.

Were it necessary a score or more mines equally as promising could be named. The foregoing will give the reader some faint idea of the wondrous mineral wealth of the Globe district.

Several shipments of ore from this district to San
Francisco have been sold at good figures, ranging
from $800 to $3,986 per ton, gold value.

The Hon. A. P. K. Safford, governor of the Territory, has an interest in some of the mines in the
district, from which ore has been mined that sold
from $400 to $800 per ton. Messrs. Newman & Co.,
Williamson, and others, have sold ores from their
mines, and one lot sold in San Francisco for the enormous sum of $11,000 per ton. Incredible as this
may be to thousands of miners who deem $100 rock
rich, the fact is well attested and strictly true. The
country is well supplied with wood and water, and
but forty miles of roadway is necessary to make it
easily approachable with loaded teams.

The district is seventy-five miles northeast from
Florence, the county seat of Pinal County, and but
forty miles from the Silver King Mine, to which a
good wagon road is opened from Florence.

The summers in the Globe district are mild and
pleasant, and the winters not at all severe, as but
little snow falls at Richmond Flat, remaining on the
earth but a short time. The snow fall is never sufficient to retard mining operations.

In the western foot hills of the Pinal Mountains,
forty miles southwest of the Globe district, and
thirty-five miles northeast from Florence, is one of
the most remarkable mines of the world. This is

the celebrated Silver King Mine, discovered March 24, 1875, by Messrs. Long, Mason, Reagan, and Copeland. These gentlemen were all honest farmers, having farms near the Gila River, below Florence a few miles. They are all men of energy, industrious and enterprising. It had been their practice for years, when their farms required no attention, to make prospecting excursions through the mountains, and when they discovered the Silver King they were on their return from the Globe Copper Mine, which they had previously located. The discovery of the Silver King was almost an accident. Hundreds of miners, prospectors, and soldiers, had passed over it, and a few years previously a company of soldiers, belonging to General Stoneman's command, encamped for weeks close by the mine. At the time of the discovery none of the locators had money to assist in its development, but they went to work with will and energy, and succeeded in developing one of the most noted mines ever yet discovered.

On the 26th day of June, 1876, only fifteen months after the discovery, Messrs. Long and Copeland sold their interests to Mason and Reagan, for the sum of $65,000 each, including the value of the ore already mined. About the first of December, 1876, Mr. Mason sold his half interest to Col. James M. Barney for $300,000, gold coin.

The vein matter of the Silver King is eighty-seven

feet wide, and the depth of working is one hundred and ten feet. The whole upper surface of the mine is worked and taken to the assorting dump for assortment and classification. The ore is assorted into first, second, third, and fourth classes. The first includes all which assays over $2,000 per ton; the second all between $1,200 and $2,000 per ton; the third all between $500 and $1,200 per ton; and the fourth all below $500 per ton.

That below $500 per ton, assay value, is saved for future working, and the three first classes are sacked and shipped separately to San Francisco and there sold. A considerable amount of the ore has been worked in furnaces at Florence, and elsewhere. The amount sold in San Francisco in 1875 cannot now be definitely ascertained. The amount sold there in 1876 was one hundred and sixty-three tons, which realized in gold coin $137,642.52, and this brought seventy-five per cent of the assay value.

There is now on the dump at the mine over one thousand tons of fourth class ore, which will work an average of $350 per ton, or in the aggregate $350,000.

There are three levels now being worked in the mine, and over $1,000,000 of ore is now uncoverd.

These rich ores are antimonial silver, nugget silver, and silver glance. When the author was last at this mine, in October, 1876, he examined one ton

of selected ore whose assay value was $12,000. H.
Kearsing, the assayer for the mine, is one of the most
competent in Arizona, or on the Pacific coast, and his
assays have never been at fault. Judge Anderson is
secretary at the mine. In the whole history of mining, there has probably been no instance where a
mine has yielded the same amount of bullion as this,
in proportion to the amount of work done.

The geological formation is granite, gneiss, slate,
and porphyritic rocks, and to the northeast near the
summit of the mountain, a thin horizontal strata of
limestone. Several other locations have been made on
the Silver King Lode, and on other rich lodes which
outcrop in numerous places, both north and south.

The Athens Mine, the first south extension of the
Silver King, is owned by Charles Brown & Co., from
which some very rich ore has been mined.

The Pike, Hard Cash, Redeemer, Silver Brick, and
Surprise mines, in the vicinity, are all promising locations. The Surprise Mine is owned by Messrs. Richmond and Welch. It is now being worked and has
yielded a considerable amount of ore which assays
$900 per ton.

There is a want of water in the Silver King district, but wood of a good quality is conveniently near,
and sufficient for many years.

There is no better opening for mining capital any-
where than in the Pinal Mountains, and the whole of

the eastern portion of Pinal County seems to be a mass of mineral, including gold, silver, copper, lead, and iron. It may be remarked that iron prevails all over the Territory, and when the demand arises, and railroads, the great civilizers of the age, traverse the country, great iron manufactories will spring up to supply the demand for mills, machinery, farm implements, etc., etc.

Pima County, which embraces the whole of Southern Arizona, is traversed by mineral veins over most of its surface in all directions.

In the Quajate [1] Mountains, south of the Gila River, there are some rich lodes of gold, silver, and copper, which have been opened the past two years, and which give promise of becoming valuable mining properties. Water being very scarce in these mountains, the work of development has been very slow, but this is now being remedied by the discovery of water at no great depth, and in a few months it is to be hoped that these valuable mines will be successfully worked.

In the southern spurs of these mountains, in the Silver Mountain district, are vast deposits of copper. This district is about fifty miles west of Tucson.

The principal operators in these copper mines are Messrs. Chas. Brown, E. M. Pearce, and Mr. Barnes. The firm of Tully, Ochoa, & Co., of Tucson, own some valuable locations in this copper belt.

[1] Qua-hä-ta.

Messrs. Brown, Pearce, & Co. own the Young America, and other mines in and around the copper peaks, some bold mountain spurs so fully impregnated with copper as to be distinguishable a distance of fifteen miles. The principal locations by these gentlemen are known as the Young America, Boston, Lafayette, Brown, and No Name, mines. These several locations have all been thoroughly prospected and worked, and large quantities of ore shipped to Baltimore, Maryland, San Francisco, and other places. Although the cost of transportation is great, they have realized fair profits on their shipments.

The ores are black and red oxides, gray sulphurets, pyrites of copper, and rich sulphurets, or salts of copper. The main body of ore, at a depth of fifty feet, is the gray sulphurets.

The ore shipped has averaged from sixty to eighty-five per cent. copper. The amount of the ore bodies seems to be virtually inexhaustible.

The formation is granite, and the mountain sides for miles around are streaked with rich though small and thread-like veins of silver ore, which has been dug out in trench-like excavations for long distances by some unknown people in the distant past. The supposition is that it was done by Indian labor under the directions of the old Jesuit Fathers, as there is in other parts of the Territory similar mining which is directly traceable to them.

Four miles west of the Copper Peaks, are some mines owned by Messrs. Tully, Ochoa, & Co., whose locations are also very rich in copper. They have taken out considerable quantities of ore, some of which they have had smelted in a common Mexican furnace with good results.

When the Texas Pacific, or Thirty-second Parallel Railroad is completed, all of these rich mines will become very valuable. Good water for drinking purposes is found near them, and a fair supply of wood.

The Picacho Mine, a very rich silver lode, is about seventy-five miles west from Tucson, and was discovered in 1860. It was worked successfully for several years, and produced a large amount of bullion. Work was relinquished when the water line was reached, as at the time there was no means by which pumps or other machinery could be obtained for working it. This mine was worked by Mexican labor, and for months before work was stopped, the water that entered the shafts and drifts was packed out by the Mexicans in rawhide buckets. The ore was worked by the Pateo process. It is known that two hundred and forty thousand ounces of silver was taken from this mine, and a large amount was supposed to have been carried away by the Mexican workmen which was never accounted for. The vein is from two to six feet wide, and paid by the Pateo process from $200 to $1,500 per ton. There are several lateral veins, or feeders, which enter the main lode, all of which are very rich. One of these lateral veins is rich in gold, as well as in silver.

This valuable mine is now the property of Don L. J. F. Jaeger of Yuma, who has lately offered it for sale at a low figure.

The Trench Mine is in the Patagonia Mountains, about seventy miles east of south from Tucson. The owners are Messrs. Archibald, Gardiner, & Hopkins of Tucson. It is an immense vein of low grade argentiferous galena ore, excellent for smelting, and easily mined. The lode is from four to ten feet wide and carries from $30 to $100 per ton of silver. Selected specimens assay as high as $600 per ton. The ore yields from thirty to eighty per cent. lead. Parallel veins of nearly equal width are within a short distance of the main lode. This is one of the few prominent mines in the Territory which have an east and west trend. Most others run north and south with slight variations. There is perhaps no better mine in the Territory of like character.

The lode has been traced and located a distance of over twenty thousand feet.

The Trench Mine, being the original discovery on this great lode, is now being worked successfully, and fifty men are in the employ of the company. Four smelting furnaces are in successful operation.

The work on the mine includes several shafts from forty to one hundred and twenty feet, and two tunnels of two hundred and three hundred feet each. Wood and water are abundant and of good quality. Iron ore is abundant and of the right quality to form a proper flux in smelting.

The old Mowry Mine, now owned by Fish, Bennet, & Co., has quite a history. It is in the southern spurs of the Patagonia Mountains, five miles south of the Trench Mine, seventy-five miles from Tucson, and three or four miles north of the Sonora line. It carries a splendid quality of argentiferous galena and carbonate ores, in a formation of limestone, ironstone, and manganese inclosed in a granitic primary formation.

It was discovered in 1857 by a Mexican herder, who sold it to Captain Ewell, afterwards General Ewell of the Confederate army, and Messrs. Brevoort, Douglass, and Johnson, who gave the Mexican a pony and some other traps for the location. In 1859, Colonel Titus and Brevoort became the owners by purchase, and in 1860 they sold it to Lieutenant Sylvester Mowry for $25.000. Lieutenant Mowry associated other parties with him, erected buildings, furnaces, machinery, etc., and worked it successfully until 1862, when he was arrested by order of General Carleton, who was then in command of the Union forces in the Territory, was taken to San Francisco, but was never tried on the charges of disloyalty preferred by General Carleton. There was much indignation among the people of the Territory against General Carleton for the arrest of Lieutenant Mowry, and it was then charged, and is yet, that the arrest was without cause, and was made on account of previous jealousies and ill feelings between Carleton and Mowry, when they were in the service in former years. Be this so or not, the result of the arrest of Mowry was the ruin of all his hopes of fortune and affluence. After his release he went to London for the purpose of selling his mine, was taken sick and died in poverty.

After the death of Mowry, his heirs, who reside in Connecticut, being either ignorant of the mining laws, or too poor to fulfill the requirements, neglected to maintain their title, and on the first day of January, 1875, Messrs. Fish & Bennet of Tucson relocated it and now hold possession. A patent has been applied for and soon the occupants will become the owners in fee simple.

The present location includes three thousand feet in length by six hundred feet in width, or over forty acres of land.

The workings now include several shafts, the deepest of which is two hundred and sixty feet, and numerous tunnels and drifts.

There are several lateral veins running into the

main lode, some of which are splendid carbonate ores. The lode, like the Trench mine, has an east and west trend, and several extensions have been located on it to the east.

The argentiferous ores work from $60 to $400 per ton in silver, and the carbonate ores from $30 to $60 per ton. Both kinds carry from thirty to sixty per cent. of lead. Much of the ore is found in great pockets, or caves, which present the appearance of having been filled by injections of the mineral from below, some of these pockets or caves being sixty feet across, all filled with mineral. A few of the caves near the surface are only partially filled with the mineral, and in them are found beautiful stalactites. The altitude at the surface of the mine is six thousand feet.

After the arrest of Lieutenant Mowry, Mexicans from Sonora carried away much of his valuable machinery, and also gouged out and took away a large amount of valuable ore, and seriously injured the mine, requiring a large expenditure of money to timber up and make it secure for working.

There are many other good mines in the Patagonia Mountains, consisting of gold, silver, and lead, and some paying gold placers.

Another rich mineral range of mountains is the Santa Ritas, west of the Patagonia Range, and divided from them by the rich and beautiful Sonoita

Valley. The **Santa** Ritas are **twenty miles** long north **and** south, **with a** width **of** three to six miles, and **they** seem to be filled with lodes of gold, silver, and **lead, in** its **whole extent.**

The district embraced **in the old** Santa Rita **min**ing district, **is in the southern declivity of the** mountains, twelve **miles east from the old** Tumacacari mission **church, and sixty-five miles south from Tuc**son.

Some of the mines in this district give evidence of having **been worked a century or more** since, **and** from traditions now current, much silver was mined here by the old Jesuit Fathers, who employed large numbers of Mexicans and Indians in the work. From 1856 to 1861, the mines here were worked by **an eastern company, but** owing to the continued and **determined hostility of the** Indians, **who** killed many **of the employees, Superintendent Wrightson and** others, **with other causes combined, work was wholly** discontinued. **Messrs. Wrightson,** ·Grosvenor, **and** Hopkins, all **leading men in the enterprise,** were murdered by the Apaches **between** 1858 and **1861.** In January, 1875, the mines were relocated under the superintendence of Col. William G. Boyle, one of the **best** informed mining men **on the** Pacific Coast. Considerable **work has** been done since their reloca**tion, but until suitable** machinery is erected for **properly working them, and mills erected for treating the**

ores, but little can be done towards their proper development. There is no doubt that with the proper expenditure of money and labor, these mines will become very productive.

In the northeastern spurs of the Santa Ritas there are numerous lodes of gold, silver, and lead, and valuable placer mines, the latter having already been described. Wood and water are both quite abundant in the Santa Ritas, but there are no large streams of water sufficient to work placers with great success.

Twenty miles west of the Santa Ritas, and forty-five miles southwest from Tucson, is the formerly noted Cerro Colorado Mine, which was worked in former years by an eastern company who expended large sums of money in machinery, and for other purposes. The lode is extremely rich, and much of the ore assays as high as $5,000 and $10,000 per ton in silver.

Like many of the early mining operations in Arizona, owing to mismanagement, incompetency, and Indian hostilities, the operations completely failed. Portions of the milling and other machinery are scattered at different places on the road between the mine and the Rio Grande River, in New Mexico, for a distance of hundreds of miles. Other portions of the machinery have been appropriated by different parties to their own use, and some yet remains, scattered promiscuously around the mine in different directions.

The Cerro Colorado Company owned another mine, the Frowita, fifteen miles south, and the two were connected by a telegraph, the first in operation in the Territory.

The Cerro Colorado Mine has been relocated by parties who are making arrangements to reopen and work it by improved processes.

The Emma Mine is a late discovery, being in the same section of country, and on a lode called the Sea Serpent. This mine is about sixty-five miles to the southwest from Tucson, and fifteen miles from the Sonora Mine. The Sea Serpent Lode has been traced and located a distance of twenty-one thousand feet. It is one of those immense lodes of mineral seldom found in any country, being from ten to forty feet wide. The ore assays from $50 to $800 per ton in silver.

The Emma Mine, which is the best developed of any on the lode, is owned by Thomas Ewing & Co., who are making arrangements for working it in a thorough and systematic manner. When fully developed, this mine, as well as the others on the lode, will produce an enormous amount of bullion.

The Ostrich Lode and Mine is seventy-five miles west of south from Tucson, and within six or eight miles of the Sonora line. It is a large, well-defined gold bearing vein, from three to twelve feet wide, with nearly vertical and well-defined wall rocks. The lode trends to the northwest and southeast, and is apparently a continuation of the old Frowita Mine. The Ostrich Mine is owned by Dr. J. C. Handy & Co. who have erected a ten stamp quartz mill which is in successful operation.

Wood and water is quite abundant. The capacity of the mill is twenty tons per day of twenty-four hours. Wood delivered at the mill costs $3.50 per cord. The company employ about fifty men at the mine and mill, paying an average of $50 per month and board for good men.

The formation is granite, with heavy dykes of slate and quartzites. The mine is in the Cerro Blanco Mountains, which extend south into the Mexican state of Sonora.

Six miles south from the Ostrich Mine is the so called Old Mine, so named from its having been worked long since by the old Jesuit Fathers.

This mine was discovered and relocated over one year since, and gives promise of becoming a most valuable property. Two well known gentlemen, euphoneously known as Hank and Yank, formerly large freighters and packers in the Territory, are its principal owners, and are developing it with much energy. Eminent success awaits them.

To the south of the Old Mine are the wonderful

Planchas de Plata, before described. These are in Sonora, a few miles south of the Arizona line.

The mines already mentioned are but few of the hundreds in Pima County. There is hardly a mountain spur or picacho peak in the county, but has its lodes of mineral, either of gold, silver, copper, or lead, and iron exists in large quantities. Scores of mineral lodes are within sight of Tucson.

North of Tucson, in the Santa Catarina Mountains, are many fine lodes of gold and silver.

Extending through the Santa Teresa, Mount Turnbull, Mount Graham, and other mountain chains, and thence south through the Dos Cabasas, and Chiricahua Mountains, are numerous rich lodes of mineral, both gold, silver, copper, and lead. Near the head of Aravaipa Cañon are many locations made by Dr. Atkinson, Mr. Buck, and others, which have been but partially prospected, but give evidence of being very rich in silver and copper. Wood and water are both abundant in this region of country, and in time, when circumstances are more favorable, many prosperous mining camps will spring up through the whole range of country named.

In the Chiricahua Mountains, in the southeastern part of Pima County and of the Territory, there has been known for a long time the existence of wonderfully rich and extensive lodes of gold and silver; but until quite recently no prospecting or mining was permitted there, as it was included in the Chiricahua Indian Reservation. This reservation having been lately vacated, prospecting parties will soon explore the mountains, and make known its hidden sources of mineral wealth.

A valuable gold mine was opened a few years since in Apache Pass, by Colonel Stone and others, a quartz mill erected, and the mine and mill were being thoroughly and successfully worked, when Colonel Stone and others were brutally murdered by the Apaches, which put an end to operations at the mine and mill, since which time no effort has been made to reopen and work it.

The foregoing brief description of a few only of the thousands of mines located and recorded in Arizona, will give the reader some faint idea of the enormous mineral wealth of the Territory. A few only have been selected from each of the many mining districts in the Territory. The number might have been swelled indefinitely, as the author visited and examined carefully nearly all of the thousands of mines located. The descriptions are literally true. and the yield of bullion, though in amount almost beyond belief, has been carefully collected from the books, certificates, and returns given from the mines mentioned, and carefully copied.

The number of mines located and recorded in the Territory, which was obtained from the county reg-

isters of each county, excepting the County of Mohave, which is given much below the actual number,
was, on the first day of October, 1876, as follows: —

Yavapai County	7,298
Pima County	975
Maricopa County	200
Yuma County	580
Pinal County	552
Mohave County	2,000
Total	11,605

It is safe to assert that the Territory is not at
the present time one half prospected, as, until the
two past years, but little thorough prospecting could
be done, on account of the hostility of the Indians.
Vast areas in the Territory are as yet almost wholly
unknown, and many sections of the country have
never been trod by white men. What will be accomplished in the coming years is, of course, a matter
of conjecture only, but judging from what has been
done the past two years from the actual results obtained, and from a careful examination of the mines
now being opened, no one can doubt that a bright
and golden future awaits those who now have, or
may hereafter have mining interests in the Territory.
What is now necessary to open up this great mineral
wealth is, first, railroads; second, capital; and third,
more men of energy, will, and perseverance, to open

and develop its inexhaustible mineral resources, and to hasten forward the day when Arizona, and its wealth of precious metals, shall be known to the uttermost parts of the earth.

CHAPTER XI.

PRINCIPAL MINERAL BELTS OF ARIZONA. — REMARKS AND SUGGESTIONS.

A THOROUGH examination of Arizona demonstrates the existence of several great mineral belts, which extend for hundreds of miles through the Territory.

The main belts have lateral branches running in different directions, some parallel with the main ones, and others at different angles from them.

One of the main belts commences near the southwestern part of the Territory, in the Colorado River range of mountains, twenty miles east of Yuma, and extending thence a northerly course through the county of Yuma, and far north, nearly, or quite through the county of Mohave.

This great belt, which is three hundred miles in length, includes the Castle Dome Mines, and many others through the river range to the east of Ehrenburg, La Paz, and the Planet, Johnson, and other mines south of Bill Williams Fork.

In Mohave County it includes the mines of the

McCracken district, the Sandy, and those of the Hualapai, Cerbat, and Peacock, and other mountain ranges.

Another of the great mineral belts commences near the southern line of the Territory, seventy-five miles south from Tucson, and includes the mines in the Santa Rita and Patagonia mountains, with a break between the Santa Ritas and the Santa Catarina mountains, and from the latter continuing north through the Santa Catarina, Pinal, Apache, Bradshaw, Walker, and Black Hill mountains, sixty miles north of Prescott, a total distance of over three hundred miles. This belt includes the Mowry, Trench, and Santa Rita mines, in the south, the Cañada de Oro, Silver King, Globe District, and other mines in the centre, and the Black Cañon, Tiger, Peck, Silver Prince, Senator, and other mines mentioned in the northern portion of the belt. This mining belt varies in width from ten to fifty miles, and it is almost safe to say that there is hardly one mile square in the whole belt which is destitute of mineral.

Another mineral belt, smaller than the two already mentioned, but equally rich, commences in the Cerro Blanco Mountains, near the Sonora line, eighty-five miles west of south from Tucson, and includes the Old Mine, the Ostrich, Sea Serpent Lode, Cerro Colorado, Picacho, Young America, Quajate, and other mines for a distance of about one hundred miles in length north from the Ostrich and Old mines.

Another mining belt commences in the extreme southeastern corner of the Territory, and includes the Chiricahua, Dos Cabasas, Graham, Cordilleras de Gila, and Steins Peak Mountains, and the Clifton Copper Mines on the north. The whole length of this mineral belt is nearly or quite two hundred miles. The lateral branches of these great mineral belts will not be specified, though many of them are equally rich in mineral as the main ones.

There is one other mineral belt, distinctively of copper, which crosses most of the others. The main ones described all have a north and south course.

The copper belt mentioned commences near the Colorado River, at the Castle Dome Copper Mines, and runs thence east for a distance of over six hundred miles, and nearly to the Rio Grande in New Mexico. This copper belt outcrops at intervals in enormous lodes, sometimes really mountains of copper, and includes prominently the Castle Dome Mines, the Young America, and others in the Silver Mountain district, the Globe Mine and others in the Pinal Mountains, and the Clifton Copper Mines in Arizona, and the Santa Rita and other copper mines in New Mexico.

The belt is from ten to fifty miles wide through its whole course.

From the foregoing brief description of the principal mineral belts of the Territory, the intelligent and thoughtful reader can form some faint idea of the extent of the mineral formation of the country.

But no one can fully realize the vast probabilities of what the future has in store for the country, without making a personal and thorough examination, embracing its geological character, its topography, soil, climate, and the many peculiarities and conditions which must ever be looked for by those desirous of studying thoroughly all pertaining to new and undeveloped countries.

After more than two years' constant and continued exploration and examination of Arizona, the author feels justified in the opinion that in mines and mining, the salubrity of climate, etc., Arizona is the *coming country* of our continent, and that capital can there be invested with more certainty of long continued and profitable results, than in any other mining section of our country.

In regard to the selection of mines, and the management of mining operations, a word of caution and a few suggestions seem to be eminently proper in this connection. Capitalists should never purchase mining property without first making a most thorough examination of the mine and all its surroundings, either in person, or through a competent and trustworthy agent. It is not safe, however, as can be testified in numerous instances, to rely implicitly on a mere book worm, either as to the value or worthlessness of mining property, no matter how high his position, or his many sounding titles conferred by colleges and universities. Scientific knowledge is all well as far as it goes, but there are a thousand things, more or less, connected with mines and mining that the mere bookworm can know nothing of but by actual experience.

The numerous instances, well known to the author, where eminent professors have at great expense examined and reported on mines, their reports costing thousands of dollars, have led to deplorable results, and ruined those who have put faith in them. The opinion of a well informed practical miner, with but a modicum of book knowledge, is more to be relied on as to the value, quality, and probable permanency of mines, than the opinion of the mere student of books without practical knowledge.

The perfection of mining is that of science and practicality combined, and this should ever be borne in mind by capitalists, and others, when looking for permanent and profitable investments, or for profits from mining labor.

Another most important matter connected with large mining operations is the selection of proper and suitable men as superintendents, financial agents, secretaries, assayers, foremen, etc. The practice of sending somebody's son, nephew, cousin, or friend, to fill any of these stations, merely to get rid of their presence at home, or to draw large salaries, is a most foolish and unwise course, unless such persons have a thorough and practical knowledge of the important duties necessary for them to perform. Hundreds of mining enterprises have failed from this course of action, which, if conducted by practical and honest men, who understood their duties, would have been eminently successful, and fortunes would have been made, where bankruptcy and financial ruin was the natural and inevitable result.

If these suggestions should be heeded, the reports of mining failures would seldom be chronicled, mining operations would be reduced to a greater certainty, and the business would be fully legitimatized.

CHAPTER XII.

COUNTIES AND TOWNS. — POPULATION, ETC.

ARIZONA is divided into six counties, to wit: Yuma, Mohave, Yavapai, Maricopa, Pinal, and Pima.

Yuma County is in the southwestern part of the Territory, and has a population of 2,212. The populations given of the towns and counties is taken from the Territorial census of July, 1876.

The county town of Yuma County is Yuma, which was formerly known as Arizona City. Its population is about 1,500. Yuma is situated on the east or left bank of the Colorado River, at its junction with the Gila River. It is one hundred and seventy-five miles above the head of the Gulf of California, eight miles above the line of Lower California, and twenty miles above the Sonora line.

Yuma is the principal shipping and commercial town of the Territory, being the point where a large portion of the goods and merchandise entering the country is unloaded from the steamers of the Colorado Steam Navigation Company. From Yuma they are shipped by wagon to Phœnix, Florence, Tucson, and the many mining camps in Central and Southern Arizona. That taken to the northern part of the Territory is taken by river steamers to Castle Dome, Ehrenburg, Aubrey, Camp Mohave, and Hardyville, and thence to Prescott, Wickenburg, and other interior towns, and elsewhere as required.

At Yuma is the Territorial Prison, which is now partly completed, and when fully finished according to the plans and specifications, will be a model of strength, utility, and **architectural** beauty. Among the other **important** buildings are the county courthouse, jail, public school-house, Catholic school-house, two hotels, printing-office, and a large number of fine stores, saloons, and private dwellings. The "Sentinel," a wide awake newspaper, is well established at Yuma, and thoroughly devoted to the interests of the county and territory. It is now under the management of George E. Tyng, Esq., an independent and thorough journalist. For several years it was under the management and control of Judge Wm. M. Berry, who was an **able** editor and a most genial gentleman.

The Southern Pacific Railroad of California will, it is expected, be finished in a few months to Yuma, when the town will receive a new and fresh impetus.

The Texas Pacific Railroad will also **cross** the river at Yuma, which will **add** much to the prosperity of the place, connecting it with San Diego on the Pacific, and with all the great cities of the Mississippi and Atlantic States.

Castle Dome Landing is thirty miles above Yuma, at which an active little town is springing up, and from which point the Castle Dome Mines, fifteen miles distant, are supplied. A store and post-office is kept here by Wm. P. Miller, who has also a smelting furnace in successful operation. Large quantities of argentiferous galena, and copper ores, are shipped from Castle Dome Landing to San Francisco. Population about 50.

Ehrenburg is a brisk town one hundred and thirty miles above Yuma, and next to Yuma the largest shipping town on the Colorado River. The population is about 300. Most of the freight for Prescott, Wickenburg, and the country east is transshipped at this town. There is a public school, Catholic church, general stage offices of the California and Arizona Stage Company. Several fine stores and private dwellings may be found here.

Ehrenburg is the present crossing of the Colorado River of the California and Arizona Stage Line, from the terminus of the Southern Pacific Railroad to Prescott, and other points in the interior. The annual sales of the merchants of Ehrenburg aggregate about $200,000. The principal firms are J. M. Barney, J. Goldwater & Brother, J. M. Castenado, and Juan Noli.

10

Mohave County is in the northwestern part of the Territory, and north of the Bill Williams Fork, that stream being the dividing line between Mohave and Yuma counties. The county town is Cerbat, a small town in the southwestern spurs of the Cerbat Mountains, and about thirty-five miles from Hardyville on the Colorado River. The population of Mohave County is put by the census at 822, but it is believed that it much exceeds that number. The population of Cerbat, the county town, is about 100. There is a good county court-house at Cerbat, a post-office, a few stores, saloons, private dwellings, etc.

Mineral Park, the largest town in the county, is six miles north from Cerbat, with a population of about 200. Mineral Park has a five stamp quartz mill, a public school-house, post-office, several stores, saloons, and private dwellings, and is the centre of a rich and extensive mining country. By act of Legislature of 1877 it is now the county town of the county.

Hackberry is a new and prospering mining town in the Peacock Mountains, thirty miles east of Mineral Park. The celebrated Hackberry Mine is the cause and foundation of its prosperity. Population about 100.

Greenwood is a fine little hamlet village on the Sandy Creek, in the southern part of the county, twelve miles east from the celebrated McCracken Mine, and the location of its quartz mill, the working of which has built up a town of 100 inhabitants. Hackberry and Greenwood have each a few stores, restaurants, and saloons, and several private dwellings, blacksmith shops, etc.

At McCracken Hill and Mine there are about 100 inhabitants, and at Planet, twenty miles west, about a score. Aubrey Landing is two hundred and thirty five miles above Yuma, and the landing for goods, merchandise, and miners' supplies, for the McCracken and Sandy districts.

Hardyville is the present upper terminus of the river navigation, and the great crossing point for immigrants from California. It is three hundred and thirty-seven miles above Yuma, and five hundred and thirteen miles above the head of the Gulf of California. It is quite an important place, being the point of transshipment of freight for Cerbat, Mineral Park, Hackberry, and other points in the interior. A fine store is kept here by William M. Hardy, Esq., a post-office, and an excellent ferry.

Yavapai County embraces the whole of central and northeastern Arizona, an immense extent of territory embracing an area of country larger than the States of New Hampshire, Vermont, Massachusetts, Rhode Island, Connecticut, Delaware, New Jersey, and Maryland, or about fifty-five thousand square miles. The population is 13,738, nearly one half of that of the whole Territory. It is fast increasing in population, and the immigrants are of the better class, consisting to a great degree of families who come to stay and to build up homes.

Prescott, the county town, and by an act of the Territorial Legislature, January, 1877, once more made the capital of the Territory, is as beautiful a mountain town as can be found on the Pacific slope. It has a population of 3,800, consisting almost wholly of white people of the better class. It is surrounded by mountains on all sides, which are covered with forests of pine and other timber. The town is well laid out on the eastern side of Granite Creek, one of the tributaries of the Verde River.

An addition has been laid out by Judge Fleury, on the western side of Granite Creek, which adds much to the beauty and growth of the town.

The Judge is an old and respected resident, and came to the Territory in 1863 with Governor Goodwin and suite, took part in the organization of the Territory, and has been identified with Arizona and its interests, and especially with Yavapai County, ever since. A beautiful plaza adds much to the beauty of the town, being in its centre, and surrounded on all sides with fine business blocks, residences, etc.

There are fourteen mercantile houses in town, three jewelers, three meat markets, four livery stables, three breweries, eight carpenter shops, eight blacksmith shops, seven wagon shops, five hotels and restaurants, five boot and shoe stores, fourteen saloons, two tin shops, two barbers, seven attorneys, four physicians, one drug store, four milliners, one dentist, one harness shop, one photographic gallery, three assay offices, one extensive sash, door, and blind factory, one church edifice, Methodist, with the Rev. Mr. Wright as Pastor, one Congregational Church organization, Rev. Mr. Merrill, Pastor, and one Methodist Episcopal Church South organization, Rev. Mr. Head, Pastor. There is also a comfortable county court-house and jail, and good county offices, and an excellent new brick school-house, erected at a cost of $12,000, and capable of accommodating three hundred pupils, with Professor Sherman, Principal, and a good corps of assistants.

Prescott has many fine business blocks built of brick, which would do credit to a large city, the principal ones being those of C. P. Head & Co., L. Bushford & Co., J. G. Campbell, Wm. M. Buffum, and others.

Prescott has two newspapers, the "Miner," the leading paper in Arizona, owned and conducted by Messrs. Marion & Beach, independent in politics, having a large circulation, and great influence. The "Miner" is daily and weekly, being the only daily in the Territory.

The "Enterprise," published by Mr. Mitchell, is a wide awake Democratic paper, having a good circulation, well edited and well supported. John W. Leonard, Esq., is associate editor, and adds much to the life and character of the paper.

Wickenburg is a small town in the southwestern part of the Territory, on the Hassayampa, and the general transfer station of the California and Arizona Stage Company. Passengers, mails, and express, are here transferred from the main line via Ehrenburg to Prescott, and intermediate stations north, and to Phœnix, Florence, and other stations south. Population 300.

Brisk little hamlet towns are springing up in all parts of the county, among which may be mentioned Walnut Grove, Williamson Valley, Walnut Creek, Peck Mine, or Alexandra, Chino, Verde, etc.

Several others are becoming quite important points on and near the Chiquito Colorado River, two of which are at the new Mormon settlements, where these industrious people are making good improvements.

There has been a large increase in the population of Yavapai County the past two years, and its increase in wealth and productiveness has kept pace with the increase in population.

During the past year Prescott exported over five hundred thousand dollars of gold and silver bullion, three hundred and fifty thousand pounds of wool, and a large amount of lumber and other products. Messrs.

Curtis and Noyes have each large saw mills near to Prescott, and both are doing a large and remunerative business.

The largest mining town in Yavapai County is at the Clifton Copper Mines, in the southeastern part of the county, which has a population on an average of 300.

Maricopa County is south of Yavapai, and has a population of 3,702. It is the great agricultural county of the Territory, and the larger part of its population are directly connected with agricultural pursuits. The great and rich valley of Salt River is wholly in Maricopa County.

The county town is Phœnix, with a population of 500. It is pleasantly situated in the valley of Salt River, two miles north of Salt River, well laid out, with a fine growth of shade trees along its principal streets, rendering it pleasant, attractive, and beautiful. In summer the thermometer ranges here from 80° to 110°, and in winter from 40° to 80°.

There are three fine flouring mills in and close to Phœnix, which furnish the larger portion of flour for Maricopa and Yavapai counties. A court-house, jail, school-house, hotel, restaurant, and several good stores, pleasant residences, etc., make up the town. The population is about one half each, white and Mexicans.

At Hayden's Mills, eight miles east of Phœnix, is

a small town with two stores, and a population of about 100.

Maricopa Wells is a noted station near the south-western part of the county, and a principal station on the great overland Southern Pacific Mail Line of Messrs. Kerens & Mitchell.

James A. Moore, Esq., one of the old pioneers of the Territory, a most estimable man, and superin-tendent of the line between Yuma and Tucson, re-sides at Maricopa Wells, with his estimable and respected family.

In the Salt River Valley, for many miles in and around Phœnix, are many interesting and wonderful ruins, the work of a long forgotten race, which will be fully described in a future chapter.

Pinal County is south of Maricopa and north of Pima, having a population of 1,600. In the eastern part of Pinal County are some of the most valuable mines ever yet discovered, embracing most of the Globe district, the Silver King, and other rich mines. The central and western part of the county, along the Gila River, is a rich agricultural country. In this valley are the Pima villages, on the Gila River Res-ervation, which embraces a large tract of valuable farming land, where the Pimas and Maricopa Indians raise large crops of wheat, pumpkins, melons, etc.

Florence, the county seat of the county, is on the southern bank of the Gila River, some fifteen miles below where it emerges from the mountains. It has a population of 500; four stores, a good school-house, Catholic church, two hotels and restaurants, one brewery, a smelting furnace, three flouring mills in or near town, and some fine residences. Shade trees,' as at Phœnix, are freely put out along its streets.

Adamsville is four miles west of Florence, the location of the Bichard Mill, the first flouring mill erected in the Territory. A large mining town is being built up in the Globe mining district, and an active one in the Silver King mining district.

Pima County is in the southern part of the Territory, and until within a few years was the most populous county in the Territory. It now has a population of 8,117.

Tucson is the county town of Pima County, and since 1867 has been the capital of the Territory, until January, 1877, when the seat of government was removed, by an act of the Territorial Legislature, to Prescott.

Tucson was settled, as claimed, somewhere about the year 1560, by an expedition fitted out by the Spanish authorities in Mexico, with whom came some of the Jesuit Fathers, who thus early commenced the work of Christianizing the Indians. It is in the beautiful valley of Santa Cruz, three hundred miles east from Yuma, one hundred and twenty-five miles west from Apache Pass, and seventy-five miles north from the Sonora line. It has a population of about 4,000, one third being whites and two thirds Mexicans. The Santa Cruz River waters the valley of the Santa Cruz, south of Tucson. This valley has a very rich soil, and portions of it have been cultivated for one or two centuries, and produce equally as well now, as when first known to our people. The town of Tucson is built up almost wholly of adobe (sun-burned brick), and to one unaccustomed to that kind of material, it presents a quaint and curious appearance. Buildings erected of this material are extremely cool and comfortable in the hot and dry climate of the country.

Tucson has two hotels, a county court-house and jail, fifteen general stores, a branch United States depository, two breweries, six attorneys, five physicians, one news depot, ten saloons, two milliners, two flouring mills, three barbers, four boot and shoe stores, four feed and livery stables, a public school-house and about three hundred pupils, a Catholic school under the charge of the Sisters of St. Joseph, with about two hundred pupils, one photographic gallery, two jewelers, several small establishments, and one newspaper, the " Citizen," edited and published by John Wasson, Esq. It has the second largest circulation in the Territory, and has done much to build up the Territory, more especially the southern part.

The business of Tucson is quite large, amounting annually to over $1,500,000. A good proportion of this business and trade is with Sonora, the merchants exchanging dress and fancy goods, boots and shoes, groceries, notions, etc., for flour, oranges, lemons, tobacco, cigars, and silver coin, of which large sums are annually brought from Sonora, where there are two coinage mints, one at Hermosilla, and one at Alamos, both of which coin from $50,000 to $200,000 per month. Tucson has ever been, and must continue to be for a long time to come, the central point for business of Southern Arizona. In summer the climate is quite hot for many months, but not unbearably so, and in winter mild and pleasant. General good feeling exists between the white and Mexican population, and a large number of white men have married Mexican women, who make kind, pleasant, and affectionate wives.

Many of the wealthiest and most successful business men of the Territory reside at Tucson, where they have accumulated handsome fortunes, in trade, government contracts, and general business enterprises.

CHAPTER XIII.

INDIAN TRIBES: LOCALITY, NUMBERS, AND GEN-
ERAL OBSERVATIONS.

THE Indians of Arizona may be classified as river and mountain Indians; as pueblo, or village, and roving Indians; as self-supporting, and non-self-supporting Indians; or as reservation and non-reservation Indians. They will be described in the order of their locality, commencing with the Colorado River Indians on the southwest.

The Colorado River Indians are the Co-co-pahs, Yu-mas, Mo-ha-ves, and the Chim-ue-hue-vas, all of whom are a large, powerful, and well formed race. They are now generally quiet and peaceable, and are easily taught the simpler forms of agriculture.

The Cocopahs inhabit the country bordering the Colorado River below Yuma, both in Arizona, California, Sonora, and Lower California. They are quiet and quite industrious, raise considerable quantities of wheat, corn, pumpkins, and melons, and cut and prepare much wood for the use of the Colorado Steam Navigation Company's river steamers, below

Yuma, for which they are paid from two dollars and a half to three dollars per cord.

They should not be confounded with the mountain Cocopahs, who inhabit the Cocopah Mountains in Lower California. The mountain Cocopahs are a wild, savage, and blood-thirsty race. The river Cocopahs number about 500.

The Yumas live on the Colorado River at and above Yuma, and number about 600. They cultivate some wheat, corn, pumpkins, and melons, do some work about the landing at Yuma, and cut and prepare some wood for the river steamers at Yuma, and for a distance above.

The chief of the Yumas is Pas-qual, an old and quite intelligent Indian, and a firm friend of the whites, whose manners and customs he often commends to his people, and urges them to adopt.

The Yumas, like most Indians, love fire-water, which, with diseases introduced among them, is making sad havoc in the tribe. They are now peaceable and quiet, unless when under the influence of bad whiskey, and great provocation.

The Mohaves are farther up the Colorado River, and range principally between Ehrenburg and Hardyville, a distance of two hundred miles. They number about 1,500. Of this number, 900 are collected on the Colorado River Reservation, eighty-five miles above Ehrenburg, and 600 are on the river above the Reservation, in the vicinity of Hardyville and Camp Mohave. The Colorado River Reservation is two hundred and ten miles above Yuma, and was established by act of Congress, March 3, 1865. The boundaries of the Reservation were extended by an executive order of the President, November 16, 1874, and it now contains 250,000 acres of land, a large proportion of which is first quality farming land. The Reservation is now in charge of Col. William E. Morford, a gentleman well qualified for the position, and who succeeded Dr. Tonner as agent, January 1, 1876. Lieutenants Fudge and Dodt, and Mr. Lehigh, had formerly had charge of the Reservation, and Mr. Lehigh was brutally murdered by his own Indians at Bell's Cañon, when returning from a visit to Prescott. Colonel Morford seems to be the right man in the right place, and it is to be hoped that he will succeed in his efforts to make the Mohaves self supporting, which has never yet been done, although large sums of money have ostensibly been expended for that purpose. It is believed by many that the money so expended has been worse than thrown away.

The Chief of the Mohaves on the Reservation is Hook-a-row, who succeeded the celebrated Chief and friend of the whites, Ar-i-ta-ba, who died some two years since. Hookarow is a large, well-formed Indian, peaceable and industrious.

The Mohaves on the Reservation receive a portion of supplies from the Government, and raise some wheat, corn, pumpkins, and melons, and gather and use large quantities of the mesquit bean, which greatly assists in supplying them with food. Aritaba, the former chief, was far in advance of his tribe in intelligence, and was once taken to New York, Washington, etc. His wonderful report, on his return to his Indians, of what he saw, of the thousand things connected with the white men, — their great cities, their great canoes, and long lines of wagons drawn with the speed of the wind by the steam horse, and the many other things he told them of, were so incomprehensible to their simple minds, they could not credit the stories, and lost confidence in him, saying the white men had bewitched the great chief.

Sic-a-hoot is the chief of the other portion of the tribe. This portion are self-supporting, and cultivate considerable wheat, corn, pumpkins, and melons; collect large quantities of mesquit beans, and perform considerable labor about the landings at Camp Mohave and Hardyville.

The Chim-ue-hue-vas are an off-shoot of the Pah Utes, and live on and about the Colorado River, and intermix, to a considerable extent, with the Mohaves. They number about 500.

All the river Indians mentioned are fond of fish,

which they take in great quantities from the Colorado River.

The Maricopas are a branch of the Yumas, which tribe they left some sixty years since on account of a difficulty with others of the tribe. They now live with the Pima Indians, on the Gila River Reservation, and will be described in connection with them.

The Mohaves, Yumas, and Maricopas speak the Mohave language, which seems to be the most perfect and original of all the Indian dialects of Arizona. That of the Cocopahs and Chimuehuevas assimilates with the Mohave.

The Hualapais[1] are a distinct and separate tribe from all others in the Territory, and now live in the mountains of Mohave County. They number 600, and maintain a miserable existence by hunting, gathering nuts, roots, and berries, and by begging and stealing. They are a small, dark race, naturally given to war and plunder. Their chief, She-rum, is a bold, bad Indian, and in former times planned and committed numerous murders among the early prospectors, miners, and immigrants. He ought long since to have been hung for his crimes.

The Pima Indians live on the Gila River Reservation, about midway between Yuma and Tucson, and with the Maricopas, who live on the Reservation

---

[1] Wal-la-pais.

with them in the most perfect harmony, number
4,326. They have from time immemorial been quite
successful agriculturists, and now raise considerable
quantities of wheat, pumpkins, melons, etc. In 1876
they sold nearly two million pounds of wheat at
about three cents per pound. They prepare their
wheat for market in a manner that would be cred-
itable to the best eastern farmers. Not a particle of
anything but the pure full formed wheat is sold by
them.

The Pimas are medium sized, well formed, peaceable, and quiet, but great thieves, stealing with impunity every article left in their reach. It is laugha-
ble, as well as provoking, to have a swarm of Pimas
gather around one's camp fire, and note with what
patience and perseverance they will steal, or try to
steal, any small article, such as a knife, spoon, fork,
or other article left on the ground. The foremost
in the circle will put his naked foot on the article,
and when he deems himself unnoticed, will give it a
throw back with his toes to an Indian in the rear,
who in like manner puts his foot on the article, and
thus it is passed from one to another until they think
it safe to pick it up and hide it in the fold of their
blankets. If caught at the game, they will laugh in
one's face with impunity, as though it was a good
joke.

An hour or more will often be passed by a score

11

or more in stealing in this way some slight article, of the value of a few cents.

The Pimas have several villages, extending along the Gila River for many miles, and have a reservation of about seventy-five thousand acres, most of which is excellent agricultural land.

The Papagoes number 6,000, and live on a reservation south of Tucson which contains seventy thousand four hundred acres of land. Their villages are near the old and noted mission church of San Xavier, twelve miles south from Tucson, and in the Santa Cruz Valley. They are nominally Catholics, and have been under the care of the Roman Catholic priesthood most of the time for nearly or quite three centuries. They are self-supporting, and have been so, as far back as their history is known; have a good supply of horses, mules, and cattle, and raise considerable produce of various kinds.

Like the Pimas, they have been friendly to our people ever since the United States acquired their country, and both have ever been ready to assist in fighting the Apaches, and at times have done good service. For reasons unknown to the author, they have lately been taken from the charge of Bishop Salpointe and attached to the Pima Agency.

Under the care and charge of the Catholics, the Papagoes have been kept free from most of the many vices which prevail among all Indian tribes soon after they become acquainted with white people, and familiarized to their manners and practices.

Why the Papagoes should under these circumstances be transferred to another agency, and no doubt be eventually habilitated with them, and where they will as a natural consequence contract the same loathsome diseases so common among the Pimas, is a matter of serious consideration, and should be carefully inquired into.

At the San Carlos Indian Agency, which is on the White Mountain Indian Reservation, are gathered most of the Apache bands of Indians. This agency is on the Gila River, near its junction with the San Carlos River. It is about one hundred and seventy-five miles northeast from Tucson.

The Indians gathered at the San Carlos Agency are the Coy-o-ter-os, Pi-nals, Ar-a-vai-pas, Ton-tos, Apache Yu-mas, Apache Mo-ha-ves, and the Chir-i-ca-huans, which include the Co-chise Indians.

The Coyoteros, Pinals, Aravaipas, Tontos, and Chiricahuans, are Apaches; and the Apacha Yumas and Apache Mohaves are a mixture of Apaches and of the Colorado River Indians. The total number at San Carlos is 4,459. Of this number 1,051 are Pinals and Aravaipas, under the chief Es-kim-in-zin; 629 Tontos, under the chief Char-le-pan; 1,512 Coyoteros, under the chief Bab-by-du-clone; 297 Chiricahuans, under the chief Ta-za; 352 Apache Yumas, under the chief Snooks; and 618 Apache Mohaves, under the chief Charley. M. A. Sweeney was at last accounts acting agent at San Carlos, and under his management the Indians are being taught habits of industry, and it is to be hoped that they will in time, at least partially, if not wholly, become self-supporting.

From Mr. Sweeney the following **Indian** statistics for the year 1876 were obtained: —

Total number of acres of land cultivated	**549**
Brought under cultivation in 1876	**221**
Number of tons of hay cut by the Indians	**350**
Number of horses owned by the Indians	**537**
Number of mules	**22**
Number of burros	18
Number of sheep	5,000
Number of cows	125
Number of bulls	6
Number of cords of wood cut by the Indians in 1876 . .	500
Number of pounds of wheat raised	10,000
Number of pounds of corn	200,000
Number of pounds of barley	28,000
Number of pounds of beans	**13,000**
Number of melons	**6,000**
Number of pumpkins and squashes	4,000
Number of pounds of mescal gathered and roasted for food	75,000
Number of Indians under medical treatment in 1876 . .	3,237
Number of births in 1876	86
Number of deaths in 1876	20
Number killed in 1876	1

The war chief of the Apache Mohaves, named Mi-ra-ha, left the Reservation July 26, 1876, without leave, and was killed by Captain Porter near the Verde River, far from the Reservation.

The White Mountain Reservation embraces a large extent of country, containing two and a half millions of acres or more. Most of this vast section of country is totally useless to the Indians and can never be utilized for their civilization, and should be opened to the use of white men.

The Navajoes [1] are also an Apache band, and occupy a reservation in the northeastern part of Arizona, and northwestern part of New Mexico, comprising 3,328,000 acres of land. They number 9,114. They are a bold, active, warlike people; sharp, keen, and shrewd; naturally inclined to rob, murder, and steal, and before their subjugation lived by war and plunder. They would often go hundreds of miles to raid on other bands of Indians, and on Mexicans, and at times would drive back from their forays thousands of horses, cattle, and sheep. They now have large bands of stock. They are very ingenious and make the most beautiful and costly blankets of any of the Indian tribes, the best of which are woven in bright and gaudy colors and many devices, and worth a horse each.

South of the Navajo Reservation, both in Arizona and New Mexico, is the country of the Zuñis, one of the most interesting tribes on the continent. The

---

[1] Nav-a-hoes.

Zuñis are worthy of special mention, and a large work could be written of them, their traditions, habits, customs, manners, religion, etc., etc.

The Zuñis number a trifle over 3,000, and they live in a large and well built town, eleven miles from the eastern line of Arizona. Their town is built on a slightly elevated hill, on the north side of the Zuñi River, and on the Zuñi arroya or plain, which runs a northeast and southwest course in Arizona and New Mexico. This great plain is eighty miles long, and from three to ten miles wide. The Zuñi River is, in the dry season, but a small and insignificant brooklet. The houses are mostly built of adobe, many of them having well laid stone floors, and plastered and whitewashed inside. The town covers about ten acres of land. The houses are erected one on the top of another, to the height of seven stories.

The Zuñis are an exceedingly peaceable and industrious people, are self-supporting, have large flocks of sheep and goats, many horses, mules, cattle, hogs, and poultry, raise large quantities of wheat, corn, pumpkins, melons, chili pepper, etc., etc., manufacture quantities of blankets, many of which they sell and trade with other Indians, and with the whites, and at times supply emigrants passing through with corn and mutton, and other articles.

Their government is patriarchal in form, and vested in thirteen wise men, or caciques, who make all the laws, rules, and regulations, for their government, appoint the governor for the town, and war, hunting, and other captains, for every general or specific purpose or enterprise.

They are a medium sized race, the men averaging about five feet four inches in height, and the women about five feet, by actual measurement of sixty or more of each sex. They are quite stout, more especially the women, are well formed, and do not have the high cheek bones so prevalent among the common North American Indians. Their language is different also from all other tribes, and their voices low and musical, quite different from the guttural of the common Indian. They are generous and hospitable to strangers, but keen and sharp in trade. Their traditions reach far back into the past for hundreds of years. One of their traditions is, that many hundreds of years since, they lived far to the southwest, evidently by their description on the great plains and valleys bordering the Gila and Salt rivers, where there are many old and interesting ruins of a long forgotten race, which will be partially described in a future chapter.

Their present town was built about one hundred and fifty years since, and near its centre is an old and venerable Catholic church, erected about that distance of time, as determined by inscriptions now legible. They had, prior to the building of the present town, seven large towns, the ruins of which yet exist, and are supposed to be the seven wonderful cities of Sibola, the location of which was long searched for by the early Spanish explorers, and which were supposed to be rich in silver and gold, so eagerly sought for by the early discoverers and explorers of the new continent. The old church is now closed most of the time, and the Zuñis report that formerly Catholic priests lived with them, but have not been permitted to do so for about sixty years past. The old church is in size 115 by 75 feet, with massive adobe walls, having a choir gallery, and embellished with a number of old paintings, now badly defaced by time.

The Moqui Indians occupy a section of country in Northern Arizona, some eighty miles north of west from the Zuñi village. They number about 2,000, and live in seven pueblos, or villages, which are upon high and abrupt table-land. They are in some respects similar to the Zuñis, smaller in size, not near as cleanly in habits, generally quiet and peaceable, but will steal. The table-lands where the Moquis live are from two hundred to five hundred feet high, and can easily be defended against the attacks of their enemies. One of these table-land plateaus is six miles long, and half a mile wide, on which are four of their villages. Three other quite small ones, have each one village. They are self-supporting, and raise corn and other produce in limited quantities on the plains surrounding the table-land plateaus.

The word moqui means death, and was applied to them by other tribes at a time long since, when the small-pox killed off large numbers of the tribe. Their original name was Ha-pe-ka.

In addition to the Indians already named, there are several small bands who live far down in the great cañons of the main and Chiquito Colorado rivers, who number in all perhaps 500. Among the number are the Agua Supais, and a few others whose names are unknown. But little is known of them, as but few whites have ever ventured into their almost inaccessible retreats. They raise some corn and other produce, and, like the Zuñis, raise excellent peaches from peach pits brought into the country, as is supposed, by the old Jesuit priests.

There are a few refugees who haunt the Chiricahua, Dragoon, and other mountains in the southeastern parts of the Territory, and perhaps a few more in the great Tonto basin, between Prescott and Camp Apache.

Of the Indians mentioned, the Zuñis and Navajoes, live both in Arizona and New Mexico; the Cocopahs in Arizona, Sonora, California, and Lower California; the Chimuehuevas in Arizona, California, and Nevada, and these tribes cannot all be enumerated as belonging wholly in Arizona. The other tribes men-

tioned make their home in Arizona, except at times
the Yumas pass some time in California on the west
side of the Colorado River. The actual number of
Indians now belonging to and living in Arizona is,
as near as can be ascertained, as follows : —

Of the Cocopahs	200
Of the Chimuehuevas	300
One half of the Zuñis	1,500
One half of the Navajoes	4,557
The Yumas	500
The Mohaves	1,500
The Hualapais	600
The Pimas and Maricopas	4,326
The Papagoes	6,000
At the San Carlos Agency	4,459
The Moquis	2,000
Small bands	500
A total of	26,442
Add refugees and stragglers	200
	26,642

The Indian reservations in Arizona cover a large
extent of country, including many thousand acres of
the best farming lands there, also large tracts of mineral and timber lands. But a small proportion of the
lands set apart for reservations can ever be utilized
by the Indians, or made to assist in making them
self-supporting. The extent of the several reservations is as follows : —

Colorado River Reservation	250,000 acres.
Gila River Reservation	75,000
Papago River Reservation	70,400
Chiricahua River Reservation	2,736,000
White Mountain Reservation	2,528,000
Navajo (one half) **Reservation**	1,664,000
Zuñi (one half) **claimed**	1,000,000
Moquis **claimed**	1,000,000
A total of	9,323,400

In round numbers this would be 14,568 square miles, a tract large enough to make a good sized state, if densely settled.

Of the Reservations above mentioned, those of the Colorado, Gila, Papago, Chiricahua, White Mountain, and Navajo, are recognized by the Government. The Chiricahua Reservation, from which the Indians were removed the past summer, has been, or probably soon will be, opened up for the use and occupancy of the whites.

The claims of the Zuñis and Moquis to reservations is founded on a claim of long occupancy and tillage for hundreds of years, and by treaties made long since with Spanish and Mexican authorities, but no official action has been taken towards a recognition of their rights by our Government. Their claims have been silently recognized by the Government, and they have never been interfered with, and most probably will not be, unless they should be removed to some more suitable locality.

The author does not desire to tread on forbidden ground, but nevertheless deems it a duty which he owes the general public, and especially the people of Arizona, to express his strong disapprobation of the present Indian policy, or more properly the want of any well-defined and permanent policy, beneficial either to Indians or the whites. The practice of setting off a large extent of country fifty or one hundred miles square, for an Indian Reservation, over which they can roam at will, encourages them in their roving, nomadic habits, and gives them opportunities for committing depredations, for plundering and theft, which they are ever ready to take advantage of.

The practice of issuing rations of beef, flour, coffee, sugar, beans, salt, blankets, and other articles, without requiring any return in labor in consideration for the same, only tends to confirm them in habits of laziness and idleness. Under this system, one half or more of the men are constantly lying around idle, basking in the sun, and living on the bounty of the Government from taxation imposed directly or indirectly on the white labor of the nation.

The idle, the shiftless, the unemployed, of all races, both Indian and white, are sure to pass most of their time in immoral practices, — in gambling and all the low vices, becoming contaminated with foul diseases, and creating cesspools of filth, corruption, and degradation, instead of being raised to a higher civilization and to habits of industry, enterprise, and thriftiness. The recognition and encouragement given to tribes and tribal relations, the keeping up of distinct organizations of petty and insignificant nations within a great nation like ours, is an anomaly in the science of government productive of no good, and much harm. Under the present treatment, the Indians become neither civilized nor Christianized, but on the contrary, contract all the bad habits of the whites, filthy diseases, become impudent, and more and more improvident, having no care or thought for their own support, knowing that Government will supply all their wants of food and clothing.

A better and wiser policy would seem to be first, to give them reservations only large enough to be utilized, to break up their tribal relations as fast as possible, to teach them that they have the same rights as the whites, and *no more ;* that it is for their own good that each head of a family locate eighty, or one hundred and sixty acres of land, with the same right of ownership as the whites have, that they are subject to the same laws, amenable the same as whites for crimes committed, and equally protected by those laws. Then teach and impress them with the fact, that after a given number of years the issu-

ing of rations will be wholly stopped, and that in the
mean time they will be taught the rudiments of an
agricultural and pastoral life.

It will no doubt take years to accomplish all this,
but it can and should be done, or some other policy,
equally as good or better, should be inaugurated, and
then the Indians will become self-supporting, which
will never be done under the present system, and our
government and people be relieved from the burdens
of taxation to the extent of millions annually. The
present no Indian policy has never made a tribe self-
supporting, and perhaps never will; has never benefited either Indians or whites, excepting, always, an
army of Indian agents, Indian traders, contractors,
and the like, who fatten on the spoils and stealings
both from the Indians and the Government.

When under tribal relations, gathered on reservations, and supported by Government, no Indian should
be allowed to leave the Reservation unless accompa-
nied by a proper guard, and then he should not be
permitted to carry arms. The present system of
giving permits to scores of Indians to leave the different reservations for days and weeks at a time, at the
same time prohibiting white men from entering or
crossing the reservations, without first reporting to
the agent his business, or the necessity for so doing,
gives great offense to the whites, and opens an opportunity for plunder and stealing by the Indians which

they are ever ready to take advantage of whenever an opportunity offers.

Neither the Government nor its agents should ever make promises to Indians unless they are right and just, and when made they should ever be fulfilled. Indians are not fools, and in many things they have as correct an opinion of right and wrong as the whites. As a general thing they are truthful, and consider that a promise once made is to be kept and fulfilled faithfully. Many of the wars, murders, and depredations committed by them, have been caused by broken promises, cheating, and frauds, on the part of the whites. Many instances could be given in Arizona, and elsewhere, to substantiate this assertion.

One instance will be given that occurred in Arizona, which was feared would lead to an Indian war, but which was fortunately avoided by the presence of a large body of troops. While in command of the department of Arizona, General Crook, who is unexcelled in a knowledge of Indian character, mode of warfare, and the proper way and manner to subdue hostile tribes, had succeeded in the complete subjugation of the Tontos, Apache Mohaves, and Apache Yumas, and had gathered them on a Reservation on the Verde River, promising them that the Reservation should be their home so long as they remained good Indians. Placing implicit confidence in the promise of the General, they remained on the Reservation peaceable and quiet, made good improvements, dug irrigating ditches, and were becoming partially self-supporting, when in some unknown and unaccountable manner, an order was issued from the Interior Department at Washington, to remove these Indians, in the dead of winter, to the San Carlos Reservation, a distance of nearly two hundred miles; a special agent was sent out to accomplish the work, and the military under General Crook were commanded to assist in doing what the General had promised the Indians should not be done. The General, like a true soldier, obeyed the orders of his superiors, though it must have been extremely humiliating to him to do so, when he and all others knew that these Indians had faithfully fulfilled their promise to be good Indians. The result was, the Indians lost confidence in General Crook, and he, chagrined and mortified, soon after was fortunately transferred to the department of the Platte, where he now is.

It is to be earnestly hoped, that our wise men in Washington will soon see the necessity of inaugurating and adopting a settled and permanent Indian policy, which will be just to the Indians, and just to our government and people; which will tend to make good citizens of them instead of vassals, beggars, and robbers; which will release the white race from unnecessary and unjust taxation, and which will tend to elevate, instead of degrading the aboriginal race of our country.

CHAPTER XIV.

PREHISTORIC RUINS OF ARIZONA.

ONE of the most interesting features connected with an exploration of Arizona is the examination of the ruins of a prehistoric race, who were evidently well advanced in civilization, and possessing many of the comforts and conveniences of civilized life. These ruins consist of towns and cities, of irrigating canals, of stone implements, pottery ware, etc., and of rude hieroglyphics and pictures of men, animals, birds, reptiles, and other objects, animate and inanimate, painted on, or cut deep into rocks in different sections of the Territory.

A thorough study and examination of all the many wonderful ruins, and of matters connected with them, would take a lifetime.

In the great valleys and plains bordering the Gila and Salt rivers, the buildings were constructed almost wholly of concrete, while those in the mountains were mostly of stone. The aceiques, or irrigating canals, were of great length and size, and conducted the water from the great rivers, far over great tracts of country now incapable of cultivation for want of water, and which must at that time have been well supplied and cultivated by that old and numerous race. The stone implements consist of stone axes, stone hammers, stone rings, stone metats for grinding grain, etc.; and the broken pottery consisted of many patterns and kinds, sizes and forms, painted and unpainted, glazed and unglazed ; some of which were of beautiful color and finish, the painting and glazing being apparently as fresh and perfect as when completed, hundreds if not thousands of years since.

The stone implements and pottery are found in large quantities in and around the old ruins, along the irrigating canals, and scattered here and there to some extent over a large portion of the territory.

A brief description of a few only of the old ruins will be given, sufficient, it is to be hoped, to awaken attention to them, and to induce some society or organization, the General Government, or some wealthy and generous individual, to take measures for a thorough exploration of them.

In traveling up the great Gila Valley, from Yuma to Tucson, many of the old ruins will be found at but little distance from the stage road. At Gila Bend, one hundred and twenty-five miles east from Yuma, and eight miles from where the Oatman family were murdered by the Tonto Indians, in 1851, are some extensive hieroglyphics, called the Painted Rocks.

This mass of rock rises from the surface of the plain to a height of perhaps fifty feet, the uppermost being a broken ledge, from which masses have fallen off, and the whole covering less than an acre of land. On the standing ledge, and on the broken masses at its base, are carved deep in the surface rude representations of men, animals, birds, and reptiles, and of numerous objects real or imaginary, some of which represent checker-boards, some camels and dromedaries, insects, snakes, turtles, etc., etc.; and on the broken rocks at the base of the ledge are found on all sides like sculptured figures, some of which are deeply imbedded in the sand. These pictured rocks present much of interest to the thinking mind, and when examined by some one versed in hieroglyphical reading, may be found to give some clue to the time of making and the people who made them.

Farther up the Gila Valley, for a distance of one hundred and fifty miles, the whole valley is covered in places, for miles in extent, with the ruins of irrigating canals, houses, towns, and cities, on both sides of the river.

In places are found the outlines of reservoirs, embankments, raised plateaus, etc., and the houses and towns seem to have been laid out with due regard to the points of the compass, as though the builders had some knowledge of astronomy, or at least of the north star.

The best preserved building in the valley of the Gila has been designated the " Casa Grande," — Great House — though in size it is much inferior to many others, but being better preserved is so called. The Casa Grande ruin is forty-five feet wide, and sixty-three feet long, and the walls now standing are nearly forty feet high, or, four and a half stories. The walls are of concrete, over five feet thick at the base, and the tiers of concrete are thirty inches each in height.

The early Jesuit Fathers who explored this country in the latter part of the sixteenth and during the seventeenth centuries, described the old ruins very minutely, mentioning also the great irrigating canals, the stone implements, and the broken pottery ware scattered profusely over the plain. Their description would well answer a description at the present time. The old Fathers could obtain no information from the then existing Indians as to who built the towns and cities then in ruins, any more than can now be obtained of the Pima Indians, and in answer to questions asked by them, they received the same answer as was given the author by the Pima Indians, which was Moc-te-zu-ma.

No other answer or information could be obtained from them, and they evidently knew no more about the builders than ourselves.

The great irrigating canal, which is near the Casa

Grande ruin, is almost entirely obliterated where the soil is of a rich sedimentary character, and can there only be traced by the broken pottery, as the canal is entirely filled by the rains and storms of past ages; but where it was cut through hard, cemented, and stony ground, it is easily traced and in places open for hundreds of yards to a depth of five to ten feet, having a width of fully twenty-five feet.

The Casa Grande ruin is on the south side of the Gila River, and nearly four miles distant from it, surrounded by a great plain from twenty to fifty miles in extent. It is about twelve miles below Florence, the county seat of Pinal County. The great irrigating canal commences some fifteen miles above Florence, where the water was taken from the river, and can be traced far down the valley towards Maricopa Wells, a distance of nearly fifty miles.

It is evident that this, and numerous other canals of like character, were excavated by a numerous and industrious people, and that they carried out the earth in vessels of pottery ware on their heads, the same as the Chinese are said to do now.

No implements of iron have ever been found in or around the old ruins, nor the bones of any large domestic animal, such as the horse or ox.

They were evidently constructed in an era of time corresponding to the Stone Age of Europe.

The vegas, or beams, which supported the upper

floors of the houses, were no doubt cut by them with stone axes, as the ends remaining in the concrete walls present that appearance.

These vegas, as well as the other wood-work of the interior of the Casa Grande, and other buildings examined, were burned out as though destroyed by an enemy, which was perhaps the case. On the north side of the Gila River, and extending a distance of many miles below Florence, are many other old ruins, some of the buildings being over one hundred feet in length, with a corresponding width.

About two miles west of Florence, on the north side of the river, between the homes of Mr. Stiles and Mr. Long, is a stretch of hard, stony land, through which another of the large irrigating canals was cut, and where, for several hundred yards, one can ride on horseback in the canal, which is yet so deep one cannot look over its banks on either side, when sitting on his horse.

Four miles to the west, on the line of the canal, are the ruins of another old town, the outlines of some of the buildings being easily traced. One of them is one hundred and twenty feet long, and eighty feet wide. It was surrounded by a wall of concrete and stone, portions of which now remain; and this wall was one hundred and thirty feet long on two sides of the building, and two hundred and twenty-five feet long on the other two sides, forming a kind of court-yard inclosing the building. This court-yard was filled in on the south and east sides with earth to a depth of four feet.

The soil in the valley of the Gila is very rich, and with the large supply of water furnished by these great irrigating canals, the valley must have been very productive, and capable of supporting a numerous population.

Sixty miles to the north of Florence, in the great valley of Salt River, at different distances from the town of Phœnix, the county town of Maricopa County, are other old ruins, more extensive than those in the Gila Valley.

In the Salt River Valley, within a radius of thirty miles, are the ruins of several large towns, some of which are over three miles in extent.

Six miles east from Phœnix, and two miles from the Hellings Mill, now owned by Major C. H. Vail, are the ruins of a large town, near the centre of which is one very large building, two hundred and seventy-five feet long, and one hundred and thirty feet wide. The debris of this building forms a mound which rises thirty feet above the surrounding plain. The walls of this building are standing about ten feet in height, and are fully six feet thick. There seem to have been several cross walls, and the whole was surrounded by an outer wall, which on the south side was thirty feet from the main wall; on the east, sixty feet; on the north, one hundred feet; and on the west side, sixty feet.

On the north, and at the northwest corner, were two wings, perhaps guard or watch houses. On the south of the outer wall was a moat, that could be flooded with water from a large reservoir fifty yards, to the south. Several other large reservoirs are at different points in and around the main town, which was over two miles in extent.

A large irrigating canal runs to the south of the large building, which was from twenty-five to fifty feet wide. This canal took the water from Salt River eight miles above, and can be easily traced for twenty miles or more below.

The people who excavated these canals must have had a knowledge of engineering, as they are cut on a true and perfect grade. Several engineers who have surveyed canals for irrigation along the line of the old ones, acknowledge that they cannot improve the grade, or gain an inch of grade to the mile.

The largest of the old irrigating canals, visited and examined by the author, is some twenty-five miles above Phœnix, on the south side of Salt River, near the point where the river emerges from the mountains. This one, for eight miles after leaving the river, is fully fifty feet wide. For this distance it runs in a southwest course through hard, stony ground, and enters on a vast stretch of mesa or table-

land, which extends south and southwest from thirty
to sixty miles, having an elevation above the river of
nearly one hundred feet.

At about eight miles from where this great canal
leaves the river, it is divided into three branches.
each twenty-five feet wide, one of which runs an east
of south course, one nearly south, and the third southwest, the three probably carrying water sufficient to
irrigate the whole of the immense plateau of table
land before mentioned. Two miles west of where the
main canal branches are the ruins of a large town
which extends along the mesa for many miles.

Near the centre of this town are the ruins of the
largest building yet discovered. Its ground measurement is 350 feet by 150 feet, with outer walls, moats,
embankments, and reservoirs, outside the main walls,
and ruins of smaller buildings in all directions.

The presumption is, from a careful consideration of
all the circumstances connected with the old ruins,
that the large building, one of which is found in
every town, was a temple, perhaps for sun worship, as there are many evidences that they were
sun worshippers.

On the line of the branch canals, distant many
miles from this one, are other ruins of towns similar
to the others described. Below the great canal and
the large ruins described, extending through what is
called the Tempe Settlement, are other irrigating

canals of nearly equal size to the others, and which were taken out of the river. many miles below the large one mentioned, and along these are also the ruins of great houses and towns.

In the Pueblo Viejo, or upper Gila Valley, are the ruins of some ten or more old towns, with irrigating canals, etc., of the same character as those in the great valleys of the Gila and Salt rivers.

Some of the ruins in the Pueblo Viejo Valley are near mountain spurs where rock is abundant, and these were built of stone instead of concrete. This beautiful valley is one hundred and fifty miles north-east from Tucson, and contains about one hundred thousand acres of choice farming land, which was evidently all cultivated by the old prehistoric race.

Well towards the upper end of the valley, on a piece of table land, elevated above the river some fifty feet, are the ruins of a considerable town, large reservoirs, some round and some square, connected by canals. One of these reservoirs is two hundred feet square, and walled up on the inside ten feet in height.

The inhabitants of these old prehistoric towns were evidently cremationists, as from time to time a few burial urns of pottery ware have been found, filled with ashes and small pieces of partially burned human bones. These cremation or burial urns were quite small, about the size of a large coffee cup, urn shaped, and generally inclosed in two or three larger ones, the largest of all being from twenty to thirty inches in diameter, and turned bottom side up over the smaller ones, thus shielding and protecting them and their contents.

The ruins of this ancient race are found over a wide extent of country, from the great valleys mentioned, for a width of fifty to one hundred and fifty miles and for four hundred or more miles in length, far to the northeast, to the country of the Zuñis.

Through this whole section of country, in almost every little valley among the mountains, are ruins of houses, towns, irrigating canals, and other evidences of their work, the buildings being almost wholly of stone. On the summits of the highest mountains, along this whole distance, are the ruins of what are supposed to have been their temples of sun worship, and perhaps also a place for refuge in time of danger. A few only of the hundreds examined will be described.

Some twenty miles south from Prescott, and two miles north from Walnut Grove, in sight of Captain Bartlett's house, is a mountain top with a walled inclosure of about two acres. The wall surrounding this inclosure is in places ten feet thick, and ten to fifteen feet in height. Inside this wall are the ruins of fourteen old stone houses.

Six miles southeast from Captain Bartlett's, on the

east side of Milk Creek, is another mountain top, three thousand feet above the little valley below, and on this summit there is also a walled inclosure, containing about five acres. The wall is very heavy and high, and inside it are the ruins of twenty-four stone buildings from twenty to thirty feet square. The ruins of a stone causeway, leading from a south spur of the mountain to the main summit, can be traced for fifty yards. It is twelve feet wide, built up on the sides with bowlders of a ton in weight, between which were filled in smaller stones and earth.

From this summit, a grand panoramic view can be had of the surrounding country for a long distance, embracing mountains, valleys, and plains.

Several miles up the Hassayampa Creek from Walnut Grove, and some eight or ten miles south from Prescott, are many ruins of stone houses, some on the high hills bordering the Hassayampa, and some in the valleys near the creek; some of those in the valleys near the creek are surrounded by large pine forests, and inside the walls of one of the ruins were three large pine trees of hundreds of years growth.

There are many ruins around Prescott, and one series is in the village just west of Granite Creek, on Judge Fleury's land. This series is on an elevated plateau, some two hundred feet above the creek, and they were originally fenced in by a large stone wall, most of which has been taken away for use in the town.

For a distance of sixty or seventy miles west there is a continuation of ruins of stone houses, fortifications, temples, etc., without number. They extend into the eastern part of Mohave County.

The ruins are plentiful around Williamson's Valley, Walnut Creek, Camp Hualapai, Mount Hope, and other places. The most prominent are on the summits of high mountains.

In Chino Valley, twenty miles north from Prescott, are some interesting ruins, well worthy a visit and thorough examination. Chino Valley is rich and fertile, contains a few fine farms, and was no doubt formerly a favorite locality for the ancient race, now unknown. The ruins extend for a long distance in and around the valley, there being a series of nearly a score in sight from almost any point in the valley. The springs which water the valley were long since used for irrigation, there being yet evidences of them to be seen.

Within less than one hundred feet of Mr. Banghart's residence are a series of ruins of stone houses, five in number, surrounded by a stone wall. The earth has accumulated around the wall and houses to a depth of several feet since their destruction, which was evidently the work of an enemy.

Mr. Banghart has partially excavated one of these

buildings to a depth of five feet below the surface. The inner walls of the room were plastered, and the walls were partly of concrete and partly of stone. On the west side he found a number of large ollas [1] filled with what was evidently burned or charred beans and corn. Near the southeast corner he found portions of three skeletons, one of a large man, one apparently of a woman, and the other of a child, and near them a water olla. They were evidently killed inside their building while defending it. Mr. B. also found nearly a dozen stone axes and hammers in excavating this room. The stone of which the wall and buildings were made was trachyte, and must have been brought from a volcanic mesa, about one mile to the west, where they are abundant.

One mile north of Mr. Banghart's is a very large stone building on the summit of a hill, which was probably a temple or a fortress, also built of stone, and the stone were square dressed.

In a cañon yet a little further north are a few small cave dwellings of considerable interest, but difficult of approach. In this cañon the Verde River takes its name, though there are some small tributaries many miles to the southwest and west, and along the Verde, in its winding course of nearly one hundred and fifty miles, are continued evidences of the work of the ancient people of the country.

[1] A large earthen vessel, pronounced O-ya.

Four miles below Mr. Banghart's, and two miles to the north of the Hon. John H. Marion's sheep ranch, is a high hill overlooking the Verde River, and a series of ruins of stone houses, inclosed by a stone wall on the south side, which in places is twenty feet high, and twelve feet wide. The other sides of the hill are abrupt and precipitous, and two to three hundred feet perpendicular.

Three miles further to the east is one of the highest mountain peaks of the country, and its summit is inclosed by three tiers of stone wall, a few hundred feet apart. Old stone ruins of an extensive character crown its summit, and here perhaps was a great temple for sun worship for many long years.

To the east of Prescott eighteen miles, in the Agua Frio Valley, on the site of the present residence of Mr. Nathan Bowers, there was a very large ruin of a stone building, which was one hundred and sixty feet square. From the debris of this building, a large double stone house, one smaller one, and much stone wall have been erected, and there yet remains on one side, a pile of debris four or five feet in height.

On the hills around are many other old stone ruins, as well as on the summits of high mountains in every direction, and for long distances.

In the Verde Valley, forty miles east from Prescott, and extending up and down that valley for long distances, are scores of stone ruins similar to those here-

tofore described.   They are found also in all the contiguous valleys of Beaver, Oak, and other creeks, on
the hills and the mountain summits, as elsewhere.

Opposite Camp Verde, a short half mile on the
eastern side of the river, are many large stone ruins
on the bluffs overlooking the river, the walls of which
are standing twenty to thirty feet high, and immense
quantities of broken pottery are strewn freely over
the ground.   Two miles down the river, and a half
mile east of it, on a stretch of table land elevated
above the river bottom one hundred feet or more, is
what was, as is supposed, an ancient burial ground.
It covers nearly one hundred acres of ground.   The
graves were inclosed by stones placed in an oblong
circular form, from two to six feet in diameter.

Beaver Creek enters the Verde River a half mile
above Camp Verde, coming in from the northeast.
This section of country is a limestone region, in which
are some of the most interesting cave dwellings to be
found in Arizona.   Beaver Creek is hemmed in much
of the distance for many miles, by abrupt, perpendicular bluffs of limestone, in which are many interesting old cave dwellings.   They are mostly walled up
in front, and at a distance look like the natural stony
bluffs.

In two of these cañons, some six miles up the creek
on the north side, are several caves some twenty feet
above the creek, in two of which are perfect cisterns,

made of cement, and almost as hard as marble, and as perfect as when made. On one of them are prints of the hands of their makers, indented in the cement while in a plastic state, and also the print of the tiny hands of a small child, no doubt made by the little one in childish glee and play. Though both man and child have long since passed away, and have been forgotten for unknown ages, the imprint of their hands remain yet to tell a long forgotten story of the unknown past. How long ago these imprints of the little hand were made, none can tell, but there they are full and fresh as when first made. The changes of time, the warring of the elements, and the upheavals and commotions of mother earth, have failed to impair or obliterate those hand pictures, and there they will probably remain for ages to come, telling their silent story of the long, long past.

Three miles below these caves are numerous others in a high bluff on the north side of the creek. This bluff is nearly or quite four hundred feet high, and is almost perpendicular.

The largest of the caves is ninety feet across in front, walled up to its very top, a distance of over fifty feet, and difficult and dangerous to enter, as the opening is nearly one hundred feet above the base of the cliff. The debris from the cave is piled up against the foot of the perpendicular wall rock for nearly one hundred feet, from which point explorers must climb the face of the vertical wall rock nearly the same distance to reach the opening to the cave. This must be done by clinging to poles and jutting points of rock, and occasionally obtaining an insecure foot-hold but a few inches wide.

When once in the cave, it is found to be divided into many rooms. The extreme height is fifty to seventy-five feet, as near as one can judge. The wall in front is laid in mortar, or cement, and near its uppermost part are two port holes, from whence the dwellers within could obtain a view of the country for a great distance around. But few whites have ever succeeded in exploring this cave, and it took us several hours to accomplish the feat in safety. When first explored there were found in it a few stone axes, metats, and other stone implements.

Continuing on to the northeast from Prescott, for two hundred miles, there are scores and hundreds of other ruins, and hieroglyphical paintings, extending to the Zuñi Village heretofore described.

From what has been written descriptive of a few of the many hundreds of ruins found in Arizona, the intelligent reader will readily concur in the opinion, that sometime in the long distant past, a numerous race of a semi-civilized people lived and occupied most of Arizona, a race far antedating the present Indians, and far superior to them in industry and intelligence, and possessed of a good degree of patient resolve, and of untiring perseverance. They must have been tillers of the soil, and peaceable and quiet in their habits. Their implements of stone were well formed, and must have required great patience and long continued toil in their manufacture, as most of them were of volcanic and other hard rock. But few insignificant implements of the war and chase have ever been discovered in or around their ruins, from which fact the inference is drawn that they were a peaceable and quiet race, more inclined to the pursuits of peace than of war.

To the present time, not one of the old ruins has been fully excavated or explored. This is to be regretted, as much of an interesting and instructive character might be discovered, which perhaps might lead to some definite knowledge of the builders, as to what race they belonged, the time when they occupied the country, and their probable fate.

It is to be hoped that an official or private exploration will soon be made of these most interesting ruins, which might result in the obtaining of some such definite information respecting the ruins and their makers, — of the interesting people who once tilled the rich soil of Arizona, and roamed through its mountains.

CHAPTER XV.

SCHOOLS AND EDUCATION.

IT will be interesting and important for those desiring to locate in Arizona to know that the Legislature of the Territory has enacted a good school, law, patterned after the best of the States east and west. This law is intended to give to every child in the Territory a thorough common-school education.

The Hon. A. P. K. Safford, and other leading gentlemen of the Territory, have worked long and faithfully to inaugurate a good common-school system on a broad and permanent basis, equal in all respects to that of the older States and Territories. The system is now well established, and with a few necessary amendments will no doubt be eminently successful. Schools have been successfully established in most of the towns in the Territory, and good and competent teachers employed who are having excellent success.

Several Catholic schools are also firmly established at different localities.

In Yuma County there are two public schools, one

at Yuma and one at Ehrenburg, and also one Catholic school at Yuma, under the charge of the Sisters of St. Joseph, which is quite successful. The Yuma public school employs two good teachers, and has an attendance of over one hundred scholars. That at Ehrenburg has but one teacher, and some twenty scholars.

In Mohave County there is one school at Mineral Park, with one teacher and twenty scholars.

At Cerbat there is a small school a portion of the time, and at Greenwood and Hackberry some arrangements are being made for schools.

Yavapai County is quite well supplied with schools at all points where there are a dozen or more scholars. Prescott has the model school-house and school of the Territory. A new brick school-house was erected the past year at a cost of twelve thousand dollars, having all the modern improvements. It is capable of accommodating three hundred pupils, and nearly that number now attend. Professor M. H. Sherman, an accomplished teacher, formerly from Washington County, New York, is principal, and is assisted by a good corps of teachers.

At Williamson Valley, twenty miles west of Prescott, they have a school of thirty scholars and a competent teacher.

At Walnut Creek is another good school with some twenty scholars, forty miles west of Prescott.

At the Verde Settlement, forty miles east from Prescott, is a good school of twenty scholars.

At Walnut Grove, on the Hassayampa, thirty miles south from Prescott, a school district has been organized with some thirty scholars.

At Chino Valley, Kirkland Valley, and Peeple's Valley, schools are already, or soon will be, established. Also at Wickenburg, in the extreme southwest part of the county.

On the Chiquito Colorado there are several settlements where arrangements are being made to establish schools, which will ere long be in successful operation.

In Maricopa County there is a good school at Phœnix, of over forty scholars, and arrangements are being made to organize several others in Salt Valley at convenient points.

At Phœnix, in Pinal County, they have a school of some thirty scholars, and a competent teacher; also a comfortable school-house lately put in good repair.

There is a first class public school at Tucson, in Pima County, with several excellent teachers and an attendance of two hundred scholars. A good school-house has been erected at Tucson, mainly through the efforts of ladies of the town, to whom much credit is due. There is a large and well attended Catholic school here with an attendance of nearly two hundred, under the charge of the Sisters of St.

Joseph, who are having good success. They are doing much to advance the cause of education within the church.

At Tres Alimos, on the San Pedro River, fifty miles east from Tucson, and at Safford, in the Pueblo Viejo Valley, one hundred and fifty miles northeast of Tucson, schools have already been organized, or soon will be. At each of these places there are twenty or more scholars.

Some effort has been made at various times to establish schools at the different Indian agencies. While the Papago Indians were under the charge of Bishop Salpointe, a school was started there by four of the Sisters of St. Joseph, and quite a number of the Papago children attended, and were making good progress, especially in writing and drawing, for which they seemed to have a natural taste. The school is now closed.

At the San Carlos agency, arrangements were made, a year or more since, to establish a school, but with what success is unknown.

At the Gila River Reservation a school was established for the Pima and Maricopa children, and several favorable reports have been made of success.

CHAPTER XVI.

RAILROADS, STAGE AND POST ROUTES.

IT is admitted by all, that railroads are the great civilizers of the nineteenth century. This being the case, it is important to know what the prospects are for railroads in and through Arizona. One of the principal objections to immigration to Arizona, and one that has for years retarded its progress, has been its isolation, and a want of cheap and rapid communication through its borders, and with the outside world. Though there are several excellent stage lines, which have been of great benefit to the Territory, and accomplished all that the best of stage lines could do, they have not filled the want, which can only be supplied by railroads. The subject of railroad building is therefore of vital interest to the people of the Territory, as well as to the people of the whole Union, for when Arizona's wondrous mineral wealth is developed, all will be benefited.

There are two great trans-continental lines of railroad projected and surveyed through Arizona. One of them is on the thirty-second parallel, and com-

monly known as the Texas Pacific Railroad route.
This railroad would enter Arizona from the east,
either north or south of the Steins Peak range of
mountains, near the eastern line of the San Simon
Valley, follow down the Gila River, or make a detour
to the south via Tucson, and thence down the valley
of the Gila from Florence to Yuma, and thence west
to San Diego on the Pacific Ocean, where there is
one of the finest bays on the Pacific coast; a bay
easy of entrance and perfectly secure at all times.
The eastern connections of the Texas Pacific would
be with the Missouri, Kansas, and Texas Railroad; the
International and Great Northern Railroad; the St.
Louis and Iron Mountain Railroad; and with numerous other lines to all parts of the Mississippi Valley,
the Atlantic sea-board, and the Gulf of Mexico. The
Texas Pacific is now completed to Fort Worth, Texas,
and work is progressing at Yuma, San Diego, and
other points along thè line of route. The history of
this railroad route is well known to the public and
need not be repeated. As to its necessity, none can
doubt. When completed, it will open up Arizona,
New Mexico, and Western Texas; will be free from
snow blockades, and will shorten the distance and
time across the continent, and become a popular and
favorite national railroad.

Another trans-continental railroad route, is the
Atlantic and Pacific, or thirty-fifth parallel route.

This railroad would enter Arizona at or near the Zuñi Village, nearly west from Santa Fé, crossing, to the north of Prescott, the Colorado River at or near the Needles below Camp Mohave, intersect the Southern Pacific Railroad at or near Indian Wells on the Colorado desert, and thence be run on the Southern Pacific Railroad track, or on a route of its own, to Los Angeles, Santa Barbara, San Francisco, and other cities on the Pacific coast. This railroad would make connections at St. Louis with all railroads from that point, north, east, and south.

Both of these great trans-continental routes would open and develop a wide extent of country through which they pass, could be worked at all times of the year, would shorten the time and distance across the continent, would cheapen the cost of travel and transportation, and would add much to the production of mining, agriculture, and grazing wealth.

The Southern Pacific Railroad of California, which is destined to be of immense benefit to Arizona, has been completed to Indian Wells for some months, a distance of less than 150 miles from the Colorado River, and, work being prosecuted with vigor, will be completed to Yuma before July of the present year. Owing to railroad complications at Washington, the public are not informed as to the route the road will take from Yuma, nor other circumstances connected with it. It will soon become the great connecting link between Arizona and San Francisco. This railroad has been pushed forward with the same energy and skill that made the Central and Union Pacific railroads memorable, is deserving of, and will surely attain success.

Several other railroads are projected in the Territory, one of which will be a most important one, and articles of incorporation have been filed in the office of the Secretary of the Territory. This is the Prescott, Phœnix, Tucson, and Sonora Railroad. It is intended to connect with a railroad from Guaymas on the Gulf of California through Sonora to the southern line of Arizona, for which a concession has been obtained from the Mexican Government, and the state of Sonora.

The Utah Southern Railroad is of much interest to Arizona, and is now completed from Salt Lake City to Nephi, 120 miles south of Salt Lake. From Nephi to Prescott, Arizona, is less than 500 miles, and when completed to Prescott, will make direct connections with the Central and Union Pacific Railroads at Ogden, and give Northern Arizona a direct outlet in that direction.

The Atchison, Topeka, and Santa Fé Railroad is being pushed forward with commendable energy, and in a few years will open another railroad outlet for Prescott and Northern Arizona.

Two great stage lines have been in operation in

Arizona for many years, and several minor ones, and horseback post routes.

The Southern Pacific Mail Line, owned by Messrs. Kerens & Mitchell, extends from San Diego, on the Pacific Ocean, to Mesilla, New Mexico, on the Rio Grande River, a distance of 850 miles, at which point it makes connections with other lines running to different cities and railroads east.

This great stage line enters Arizona on the west, at Yuma, and on the east at the Steins Peak Mountains, fifteen miles east from Apache Pass. It is a tri-weekly route, and is made in eight days from San Diego to Mesilla. The line is well stocked with horses, Concord coaches, and closed buckboard carriages. Good Concord coaches are run over most of the route.

The coaches are run promptly on the schedule time prescribed by the Government. The proprietors, superintendents, and employees, on the route, are well informed, affable, and attentive to every duty, and, as a consequence, travel and transportation over the route has much increased the past two years. It is a very popular route, and well patronized.

The California and Arizona Stage Line is the other great stage line of Arizona. The line now connects with the Southern Pacific Railroad at Indian Wells, runs thence to Ehrenburg on the Colorado River, thence to Wickenburg, from whence the main line

runs to Prescott and intermediate stations, and a
branch line to Phœnix and Florence, where it inter-
sects the Southern Pacific Mail line before mentioned.
Both the main and branch lines are tri-weekly. An
effort is now being made to make the main line from
Prescott to the railroad a daily route, with prospects
of success.

·Another route, run by the California and Arizona
Stage Company, is a weekly, from Prescott via Mineral Park and Cerbat to Hardyville, on the Colorado
River. Petitions have been forwarded to increase this
to a tri-weekly route. The officers of the California
and Arizona Stage Company are Mr. James Stewart,
President, and Dr. J. H. Pierson, Secretary. Messrs.
Thomas and Nichols, Superintendents, are both good
men, and employ none but first class drivers.

The two stage companies above mentioned have,
for many years, kept up their several lines under the
greatest difficulties imaginable, and with hardly a
day's interruption. During the long years of the
Indian wars, their coaches were often attacked by
the savage foe, coaches rifled and burned, stock killed
or driven off, employees murdered, and great pecu-
niary damage sustained in addition to loss of life, yet,
through all these difficulties and dangers, they, with
indomitable will and courage, fulfilled their obliga-
tions to the government and people, kept up their
several lines, and are deserving the thanks and grati-
tude of all in Arizona.

These two stage companies employ four hundred horses, one hundred men, and fifty coaches.

There is a weekly stage line from Tucson, running south into the Mexican state of Sonora, and thence to Guaymas on the Gulf of California.

A tri-weekly stage line runs from Phœnix to Camp McDowell, thirty-five miles. Another one runs from Phœnix to Maricopa Wells, connecting the two first described main lines — the distance is thirty miles.

A weekly stage line runs from Prescott, via the Chiquito Colorado and Camp Wingate, to Santa Fé in New Mexico. This will soon be made a tri-weekly route.

A horseback mail route is run from Camp Grant, via old Camp Goodwin and Safford, to the Clifton Copper Mines. At Camp Goodwin it is intersected by a military post rider, who takes the mail via San Carlos to Camp Apache. From Camp Apache, the military post route runs north to the Chiquito Colorado, connecting with the line from Prescott to Santa Fé.

Another horseback mail route runs from Yuma, via Castle Dome, Ehrenburg, Colorado River Reservation, Aubrey, and Camp Mohave, to Hardyville.

Another one runs from Cerbat and Mineral Park, via Stone's Ferry of the Colorado River, to Pioche, Nevada.

Another route has lately been established which

supplies Greenwood, McCracken, the settlements on the Sandy Creek, and a few other places.

Another horseback route is from Prescott, via the Peck Mine, Bradshaw, and Walnut Grove, to Wickenburg.

The great increase in population, the springing up of numerous and successful mining towns and camps, demand increased mail facilities in different parts of the Territory, which requires constant attention on the part of the present efficient Delegate in Congress, and which he is ever willing to give.

CHAPTER XVII.

COLORADO STEAM NAVIGATION COMPANY.

THIS is the only line of steamers running to Arizona. It is intimately connected with the history and prosperity of the country, has done much to build it up, for many long years supplied most of the wants of both the citizens and the military, and is justly deserving of a longer and more extended notice than can be given in these pages.

In 1852 Captains George A. Johnson, B. M. Hartshorne, and A. H. Wilcox organized a company under the firm name of George A. Johnson & Co., for the purpose of transporting passengers and freight to and from San Francisco, Cal., and the Colorado River in Arizona, stopping at the Mexican ports of La Paz, Mazatlan, and Guaymas. They first employed sail vessels on the ocean, and in July, 1871, they put on their first ocean steamer, which was soon after increased to two. Some years subsequent to its first organization, the company was incorporated under the laws of California, under the name it now bears.

One of the ocean steamers leaves **San Francisco** every twenty days, running to the head of the Gulf of California, a distance from San Francisco of **nineteen** hundred **miles.** At the head of the gulf the passengers and freight are transshipped to four river steamers, and **taken thence up the Colorado River to Yuma, one** hundred **and seventy-five miles,** and **thence portions are taken up the river to their several** destinations. **The river steamers make regular trips to** Hardyville, three hundred **and thirty-seven miles above** Yuma, and five hundred **and thirteen** miles above the mouth of the river.

The Company have now four river steamers of four hundred tons each, and four barges of eight hundred tons.

The river steamers are the *Mohave*, *Gila*, *Cocopah*, and *Colorado.* Captains: **J. A. Mellen,** William **Poole, S. Thorn, and A. D. Johnson. The ocean** steamers **were the** *Newbern*, **Capt. William Metzger,** and the *Montana*, **Capt.** George **M. Douglass. The** *Newbern* was burned at sea in **December last, the** only serious calamity that has happened to the **Company since its organization. The** *Newbern* will be replaced with a new boat.

The officers of the Company are as follows : —

President, **B. M.** Hartshorne, San Francisco.
General Agent, **John** Birmingham, San Francisco.
Superintendent, Isaac Polhemus, Jr., Yuma.

14

Yuma Agent, A. J. Finlay.
Ehrenburg Agent, P. M. Fisher.
Mazatlan Agent, Señor Kelton.
La Paz Agent, Señor Viosco.
Guaymas Agent, Señor Willard.
General office, 10 Market St., San Francisco, California.

This Company have occupied a position, in supplying the necessities of the Territory, which could not have been filled in any other manner. For many years the citizens and military of Arizona have received almost all their supplies of provisions, goods, machinery, arms, etc., etc., through the medium of this Company, and could have obtained them in no other way.

The amount of freight brought to Yuma, in the year 1875, was over four thousand five hundred tons. The amount of freight shipped from Yuma was: —

Mineral Ores	1,000 tons.
Wool	60 tons.
General Merchandise	60 tons.
No. of Hides	6,170 tons.
No. of Pelts	1,400 tons.
Way Freight	1,440 tons.

Also a large amount of bullion and other articles.

The amount received and shipped during the year 1876 is not yet reported.

The Company have a good ship-yard on the Sonora side of the Gulf of California, where their river steamers were constructed, and where their repairs are made.

CHAPTER XVIII.

NEWSPAPERS.

THERE are four newspapers in Arizona, one of which is daily and weekly; the others are weekly. They are the " Miner," daily and weekly; the " Citizen," " Sentinel," and " Enterprise."

The " Miner " was first issued March 9, 1864, by the Hon. John H. Marion, one of its present owners and editors. Mr. Marion published it until March, 1875, when he sold it to T. J. Butler, Esq., who resold it to Messrs. Marion & Beach, the present proprietors and editors, in December, 1876. The " Miner " has the largest circulation of any paper in the Territory, has ever been ably edited, and has done much to build up the interests of the Territory, and especially of the northern part. It is published daily and weekly at Prescott.

The " Citizen," a weekly, is edited and published by John Wasson, Esq., at Tucson. Mr. Wasson started the " Citizen " some six years since, and through its columns has done much for Southern Arizona. The " Citizen " is second in circulation, is well edited and well supplied with interesting local matter.

The " Enterprise," a weekly, is published at Prescott, by C. F. Mitchell, Esq., a printer of much experience, and is edited by Messrs. J. W. Leonard and C. F. Mitchell. It is a neat, spicy sheet, and bound to succeed under the present able management.

The "Sentinel" is located at Yuma. It has been published for several years by Judge Wm. J. Berry, an able editor, who lately sold it to George E. Tyng, Esq., its present enterprising editor. It has a good circulation, is the special shipping paper of the Territory, and devoted to the interests and prosperity of Yuma County.

Of the four papers, the " Miner " is independent in politics, the "Enterprise " is Democratic, the " Citizen " Republican, and the "Sentinel " independent.

Arrangements are being made to start a Democratic paper at Tucson. Phœnix and Florence are both in hopes of having each a paper at no distant day.

CHAPTER XIX.

THE present telegraphic lines have all been built by the Military and Signal Service Departments.

The main line is from San Diego, California, to Yuma, and thence to Maricopa Wells, Phœnix, Florence, Tucson, Prescott, Wickenburg, Camps Whipple, Verde, McDowell, Lowell, Grant, Apache, Bowie, and other points.

From Camp Apache a line is now being constructed, via Camp Wingate, to Santa Fé, New Mexico.

These lines are all under the charge and superintendency of Lieutenant Read, who is a most efficient gentleman, and well qualified for his important position.

The total length of the telegraph lines in the Territory will approximate to one thousand miles.

The citizens, and particularly the military of the country, have been greatly benefited by their construction. The charges for transmission of news are very moderate, less than the charges on the great incorporated telegraph lines of the States east. This fact, together with their good management, the care, promptness, and order, with which they are conducted, gives eminent satisfaction to all classes of people.

CHAPTER XX.

MILITARY, AND MILITARY POSTS.

THERE are ten military posts belonging to the Department of Arizona, commanded by Colonel August V. Kautz, Colonel of the Eighth U. S. Infantry, Brevet Major-general, U. S. A.

Fort Whipple, Department Headquarters, is one mile north from Prescott, in latitude 34° 30′ north, and longitude 35° 30½′ west from Washington.

Fort Whipple was first located at Chino Valley, twenty-two miles north from Prescott, in 1863, and removed to its present site in 1866. Capacity of the fort, two companies of cavalry, and one of infantry. Altitude six thousand feet. Commandant of Post, Lieutenant-colonel J. D. Wilkins of the Eighth Infantry.

Camp Verde is in the Verde Valley, forty-two miles nearly east from Prescott. Camp established in 1864. Altitude 3,500 feet. Latitude 34° 34′ north, longitude 35° west from Washington. Capacity four companies. Commandant, Captain George M. Brayton, Eighth Infantry. Company B of Indian Scouts, forty strong, with Al. Seiber, guide and scout, is attached to Camp Verde.

Camp McDowell is thirty-five miles east from Phœnix, a two company post, situated in latitude 33° 40' north, longitude 34° 40' west from Washington. Commandant, Captain Augustus W. Corliss, Eighth Infantry.

Camp Mohave is on the Colorado River, 325 miles above Yuma, and ten below Hardyville, in latitude 35° 24' north, longitude 37° 35' west from Washington. Established in 1858. Capacity, three companies. It is a pleasant and agreeable post, on a high bank overlooking the Colorado River, and about one hundred and ninety miles nearly west from Prescott. Commandant, Major Henry R. Mizner.

Camp Lowell is on the Rillito [1] Creek, six miles east from Tucson. Capacity, four companies. Latitude 32° 12' north, longitude 33° 52' west. Altitude 2,200 feet. Commandant, Captain John N. Andrews, Eighth Infantry.

Camp Bowie was established in 1863, and for many years it was one of the most important posts in the Territory, being surrounded by hostile Indians. It is in the noted Apache Pass, one hundred miles east from Tucson. Latitude 32° 41' north, longitude 32° 25' 30" west. Capacity, three companies. Commandant, Captain Curwen B. McLellan of the Sixth Cavalry.

[1] Ri-ye-to.

Camp Apache is in the White Mountain country, well towards the east line of the Territory, an isolated post, but one of the most pleasant on the continent. It is on the south bank of White River, which is well stocked with mountain trout, and in a section of country abounding in bear, deer, and wild turkeys. Altitude about 6,000 feet. Commandant, Captain Frederick D. Ogilby of the Eighth Infantry. Capacity four companies.

Camp Grant, headquarters and band of the Sixth Cavalry, is located at the base of Mount Graham, in latitude 32° 48′ north, longitude 32° 38′ west. Capacity three companies. Commandant, Major Charles E. Compton, Sixth Cavalry.

Fort Yuma is on the California side of the Colorado River, opposite Yuma. It is on a bluff one hundred feet above the river, having an altitude of 260 feet. Latitude 32° 23′ north, longitude 37° 36′ west. Capacity three companies. Commandant, Major Thomas S. Dunn of the Eighth Infantry.

Camp Thomas is a new post, on the Gila River, near old Camp Goodwin. One company is stationed here under the command of Captain C. M. Baily, Eighth Infantry.

Company A, Indian Scouts, is posted at Camp Apache, and Company C at Camp Bowie.

In addition to the regular posts, there are four supply depots belonging to the Department of Arizona, as follows : —

San Diego, California, Ordnance Stores, under the charge of Sergeant Michael Donovan.

Whipple Depot, in charge of Captain John Simpson, A. Q. M., Assistant Depot Quartermaster.

Yuma Depot, in charge of Captain George W. Bradley, Depot.Quartermaster.

Ehrenburg Depot, in charge of Second Lieutenant A. G. Tassin, A. A. Q. M. and A. C. S.

The officers of the Military Department of Arizona are good and true men, and will compare favorably with those in any other department. The character of most of them is above reproach, and in this respect the Commandant of the Department sets an example to his inferiors worthy of imitation.

The officers not specially named as commandants of the several military posts are as follows : —

Colonel August V. Kautz, Eighth Infantry, Brevet Major-general U. S. Army, Commanding the Department.

Personal Staff.

First Lieutenant F. A. Whitney, Eighth Infantry, Aid-de-camp.

First Lieutenant E. D. Thomas, Fifth Cavalry, Aid-de-camp and En. Officer.

First Lieutenant G. S. Anderson, Sixth Cavalry, Aid-de-camp.

Department Staff.

Major James P. Martin, Assistant Adjutant-general, Prescott, A. T.

First Lieutenant Thomas Wilhelm, Adjutant Eighth Infantry, Acting Assistant Adjutant-general, Prescott, A. T.

Major James Biddle, Sixth Cavalry, Acting Assistant Inspec-
tor-general, Prescott, A. T.

Major C. A. Reynolds, Q. M., Chief Quartermaster, Prescott,
A. T.

Captain Thomas Wilson, Com. of Sub., Chief Commissary of
Subsistence, Prescott, A. T.

Surgeon James C. McKee, Medical Director; Prescott, A. T.

Major Rodney Smith, Paymaster U. S. A., Chief Paymaster,
Prescott, A. T.

Quartermaster's Department.

Captain George W. Bradley, A. Q. M., Depot Quartermaster,
Yuma, A. T.

Captain G. C. Smith, A. Q. M., Post Quartermaster, Camp
Grant, A. T.

Captain James H. Lord, A. Q. M., Disbursing Officer, Tucson,
A. T.

Captain John Simpson, A. Q. M., Assistant Depot Quartermaster, Whipple, A. T.

Medical Department.

Assistant Surgeon Henry M. Cronkhite, Post Surgeon, Camp
Verde, A. T.

Assistant Surgeon Leonard Y. Loring, Post Surgeon, Fort
Yuma, Cal.

Assistant Surgeon J. C. Worthington, Post Surgeon, Fort
Whipple, A. T.

Assistant Surgeon Walter Reed, Post Surgeon, Camp Lowell,
A. T.

Assistant Surgeon J. de B. W. Gardiner, Post Surgeon, Camp
Apache, A. T.

Assistant Surgeon R. L. Rosson, Post Surgeon, Camp Grant,
A. T.

Assistant Surgeon H. G. Burton, Post Surgeon, Camp Bowie,
  A. T.

Pay Department.

Major James R. Roche, Paymaster, Tucson, A. T.
Major William M. Maynadier, Paymaster, Yuma, A. T.

Post Chaplains.

Alexander Gilmore, Fort Whipple, A. T.
Preston Nash, Camp Lowell, A. T.

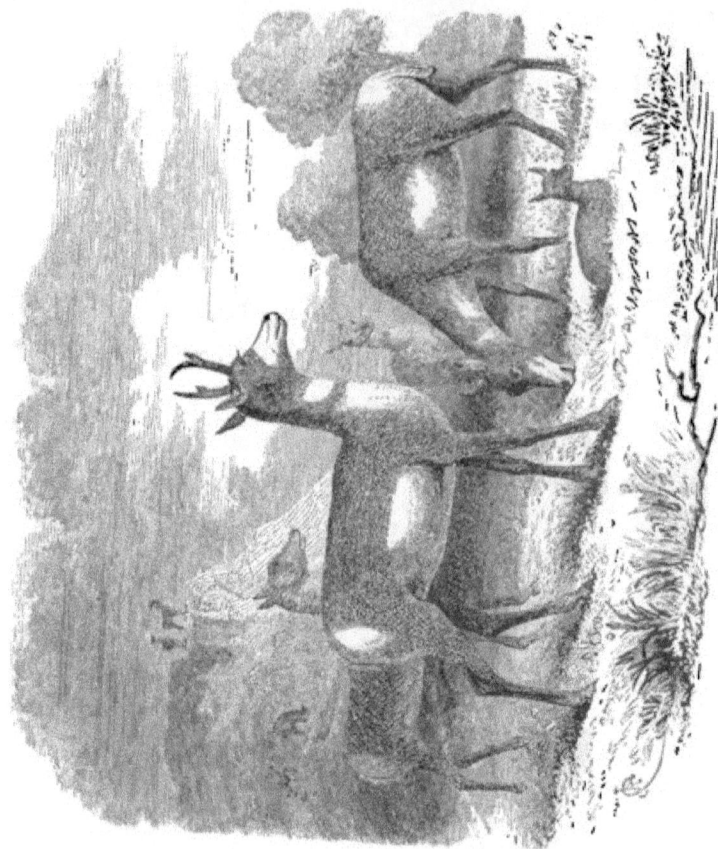

ANTELOPES.

CHAPTER XXI.

WILD ANIMALS, BIRDS, FISH, ETC.

THE most common wild animals of Arizona are the bear, elk, deer, antelope, wild goat, cougar or California lion, wolf, fox, wild cat, prairie dog, hare, rabbit, skunk, squirrel, beaver, mink, muskrat, etc., etc.

The different varieties of bear are the cinnamon, brown, black, and now and then a grizzly. The first three kinds are very numerous in all the mountainous parts of the country. The cinnamon bear is nearly as large as the grizzly bear, and a tough customer for a solitary hunter to meet.

Elk are abundant in the region of the San Francisco, Bill Williams, and some portions of the White Mountains. They are generally large and in good condition.

There are three kinds of deer, all of which are very abundant in the mountains and foot hills. One kind is the white-tailed deer, common to the Northwestern States. A second kind is the common black-tailed deer of the Rocky and Sierra Nevada mountains. A third is also a black-tailed deer, but much larger, approximating in size to the elk, and commonly called the burro deer.

Antelopes are very abundant in the valleys and plains bordering the foot hills of the mountains.

The wild goat, or Rocky Mountain sheep, is quite plentiful in some of the mountainous districts, but as they are very timid at the approach of civilization, will, in a few years, become exterminated.

Cougars, or California lions, are not very numerous, but are occasionally found in the rocky fastnesses of the mountains.

The large gray wolf is occasionally found, but not in large numbers. The common coyote wolf is found everywhere in great numbers. They are a dirty, sneaking, ill-looking animal, without the bravery to attack a man, unless in large packs, and in a starving condition.

Foxes of different kinds are found only in small numbers.

Several varieties of the wild cat are found, and among the number, a curious and interesting one, somewhat resembling the civet cat of India.

Prairie dogs are not numerous, and are found in the largest numbers in the northern part of the Sulphur Springs Valley, both north and south from Camp Grant.

Hares and rabbits are numerous over the whole of the Territory.

PRAIRIE DOGS.

The skunk and squirrels of different kinds are found in limited numbers in all sections.

Beaver, mink, and a few other fur-bearing animals are found to some extent in most of the rivers and mountain streams. Their furs are not as valuable as further north.

Other kinds of animals of rare species are occasionally found, but not in large numbers.

The most common of the birds of Arizona are eagles, wild turkeys, grouse, quail, mocking birds, pelicans, herons, sand-hill cranes, wild geese, brant, wild ducks, wild pigeons, turtle doves, robins, blue jays, larks, and a great variety of smaller birds, and numerous quantities of vultures, hawks, crows, ravens, etc., etc.

Eagles are found in the higher mountains. Wild turkeys are found in mountainous districts, but more abundantly in the northern and eastern portions of the Territory. Many of them are of great size, often weighing forty or more pounds. They are always in good condition.

Grouse are only found in a few mountainous districts, and then in small numbers.

There are three varieties of quail, some of which are very numerous. One variety is similar to the Bob White quail of the eastern slope, and the two others are similar to the top-knot quail of California, but one is much larger.

The mocking-bird[1] is quite numerous in most parts of the Territory. Its notes, both in the wild and tame state, rival those of all others of the feathered songsters.

Pelicans, herons of different kinds, sand-hill cranes (called in Arizona the Colorado turkey), wild geese, brant, and ducks, are found in large numbers along the great rivers, and geese and ducks elsewhere in lakes, ponds, and mountain streams.

Most of the other birds, large and small, are found generally throughout the Territory.

The chaparral cock, or California road runner, is found generally through the Territory. It is a tall, slender bird, weighing about one pound, is a fast runner, and does not fly to any distance. Wonderful stories are told of its fights with the rattlesnake, which it is said to surround with branches of cactus to prevent its getting away, and then kill it by continued and persistent attacks.

There is also a small bird, no larger than the wren, which is called the rattlesnake-killer, and which it is asserted pursues the same tactics as the road runner in the destruction of the rattlesnake.

Many fine specimens of the birds of Arizona, with a description of their habits, etc., can be seen in the Smithsonian Institute at Washington.

The varieties of fish in Arizona are not numerous, although the streams are well stocked.

[1] *Turdus polyglottus* of Linnæus.

˙ In the Colorado and Gila rivers are large quantities of what are called the Colorado and Gila River salmon, an excellent fish, but quite different from the salmon of California and Oregon, more resembling the cod of the Atlantic Coast. Varieties of the bass and perch are also abundant. The mountain streams have smaller fish, but similar to those of the large rivers, and in the upper branches of Salt River, the White and Black rivers and their tributaries, are large quantities of the mountain trout, where the admirers of Isaak Walton can find rare sport and enjoyment seldom surpassed.

15

R EPTILES and venomous insects are not as numerous in the Territory as has been generally
reported, and instances of serious results from bites
or stings are very rare.

There are three varieties of the rattlesnake, one
being the large black rattlesnake usually found in the
rocky gorges of the mountains. Another kind is the
large yellow rattlesnake found in low lands, and on
the sandy plains. These two kinds are from three to
five feet in length. Another kind, called the side
wiper, from its peculiar habit of locomotion sideways,
instead of ahead, is found through most of the valleys
and plains, and is from two to three feet in length.
It is quite spiteful, active, and venomous.

There are many varieties of the saurian lizard
species, resembling those found on the continent elsewhere. There is one variety, however, peculiar to
Arizona, found principally in the Gila River valley,
and locally known as the Gila monster.

It is from fifteen to thirty inches long, a dull,

filthy looking reptile, with black mouth and tongue, seemingly harmless and inoffensive. The Indians, however, say that its breath will cause one to die, but this is perhaps apocryphal.

The tarantula, which is a large black spider, the *Lycosa tarantula*, is found in moderate numbers in all the warmer portions of the Territory. Its bite is not as dangerous as generally supposed, though it is quite poisonous and painful.

The centipede, of the genus Scolopendra, is found in the tropical valleys of the Territory, where they often are four to six inches long. When they crawl over the flesh of a person, it causes a stinging, smarting sensation, quite painful, and in sensitive parts of the body would be somewhat dangerous.

The scorpion is found in limited quantities, and its sting is painful but not necessarily dangerous.

Turtles are found along the Colorado and Gila rivers of considerable size, sometimes twenty inches across. Their flesh is quite palatable.

The tarantula bug is about the size of a humming-bird, and is so named from its tenacity in the destruction of the tarantula and its nest and eggs.

The common house-fly, *Musca domestica*, is numerous in all parts of the Territory, and a great nuisance.

For about two months before the summer rainy season, some of the mountain districts swarm with large, venomous flies, which are extremely irritating to horses and cattle.

There are many kinds of bugs, insects, etc., much too numerous to mention, and of no particular interest to the common reader.

CHAPTER XXIII.

NATURAL CURIOSITIES. — GRAND SCENERY, ETC.

A MINUTE and full description of the grand scenery, and wonderful natural curiosities of Arizona, would fill volumes, and would be of exceeding interest to all who love to read descriptions of nature's works, or who delight in nature's wonderful domain. But few of these can be described in this work, and they in a brief manner only.

There are numerous cañons in the Territory, of great depth and extent. These are deep gorges, worn out by the erosion of running water, during the countless ages of the unknown past. They are grand and sublime to the highest degree. They are often many miles long, with abrupt and precipitous wall rocks on either side, thousands of feet in height.

The Grand Cañon of the Colorado, which is in Northern Arizona, is three hundred miles in length, and there are but few places in the whole distance where men can enter or emerge from its wonderful depths. This cañon has been worn through the hard granite, limestone, slate, trachyte, and other hard rocks, to a great depth. It can only be explored by entering it from its upper end, in Southern Utah, in boats prepared for the purpose, as did Major Powell and party in 1869, and then it is a most dangerous undertaking, fraught with a thousand dangers to life and limb. This grand cañon has no equal in the world, and when once seen can never be forgotten. For grandeur and sublimity, it has never been excelled by nature in her wildest moods. The description given of it by Major Powell, of the many scenes and incidents which occurred during the passage through its wonderful recesses, of the dangers to be overcome, as day by day they floated down with the rapid current of the Colorado, the falls and whirlpools met with, and overcome by almost superhuman energy and determination, the narrow escapes from death, and the many dangers encountered, — it is all of the most thrilling character. For a full description the reader is referred to Powell's reports to the Department at Washington. Entering the Grand Cañon at many different points, are lateral cañons of equal height as the main one, some of which are so narrow, it would seem that one could leap from side to side across the chasm. That of the Chiquito Colorado is the largest of the lateral ones.

In passing down the Colorado, after emerging from the Grand Cañon, several others are met with of from five to twenty miles in length, and of great interest to the explorer.

From Stone's Ferry of the Colorado River, which is 640 miles above its entrance to the Gulf of California, explorers can go down the Colorado in a strong open boat in comparative safety; and from Hardyville down, a distance of 513 miles, the river steamers of the Colorado Steam Navigation Company make regular trips. A trip up and down the river on one of these steamers is of exceeding interest, and the explorer and traveler, who visits that far off country, should by all means make the journey, which will occupy but one or two weeks. Three cañons are passed on the way, one of which is the Black Cañon of the Needles, thirty miles below Camp Mohave. It is nearly twenty miles long, and as the staunch steamer rushes with the speed of the race horse through the rushing, roaring whirlpool of waters, turning now to the right, and now to the left, under the guidance of Captain Mellen and the pilot, one looks on with bated breath, catching here and there visions of almost every conceivable object in the worn and eroded rocks on either hand, sometimes a minaret, tower, or steeple, and anon the image of some giant Titan, as if carved by the hand of man. After passing this cañon the steamer enters the beautiful Chimuehueva Valley, which opens up to the view a scene of quiet beauty, where all nature seems quiet and serene. The raging waters of the cañon above are now still and smoothly flowing, presenting a contrast to the wildness and grandeur above, quieting to the nerves, and soothing one into silent meditation, and peaceful thought.

The Bill Williams Cañon below Aubrey, and the Picacho Cañon above Castle Dome, are similar in character to the Black Cañon, though not so exceedingly wild, grand, or picturesque.

There are scores of other cañons in the Territory at almost every point in the mountains, and the mountain plateaus. Some of them are found where no permanent streams now exist, but where evidently there were in ancient times rivers of some magnitude. Others are found in the mountain plateaus where, at a distance, the smooth surface is apparently level and unbroken, and where the course of the explorer is suddenly checked by one of these great cañons, which it is impossible to pass without making a detour of many miles; others again are found where a tiny trickling stream of water runs through its length for many miles, a stream hardly deep enough to cover a lady's shoe.

One of the most interesting of these is the Aravaipa Cañon, one hundred and twenty miles from Tucson. It is eighteen miles long, and the wall rock rises in places from one thousand to three thousand feet perpendicular. A tiny brooklet, the Aravaipa Creek, runs through its whole distance, with deep pools in places, well stocked with fish. When once in the cañon, it is next to impossible to get out until one goes to the extreme end, or retraces his way to the point of entrance. It is in a few places one hundred yards wide, and again not over one hundred feet. A few lateral cañons enter it of equal depth, but only a few feet wide, from the depths of which, in looking upwards, one can see what would be vulgarly called a crack or hole in the sky, with a sight above of stars at noonday.

Occasionally a large cinnamon bear will be met in this cañon, which it would be well to avoid, also a flock of wild turkeys, one of which would make a choice meal for a number of hungry men. A few chaparral bushes and cottonwood trees grow in places in the cañon, and far up in the cliffs of the overhanging rocks, specimens of the giant cactus, the *Cereus giganteus*, spread out their giant arms as if in wonder at the scene below.

The mountainous parts of Arizona, which comprise nearly or quite two thirds of its area, are literally cut up and filled with these wonderful gorges, some of which have never yet been explored by white men, and which would require years of time to fully explore. The formation is generally granitic, with occasional heavy dykes of hard lime and sandstone, slate, porphyry, and in places trachyte, through whose hardened surfaces these chasms have been worn in the lengthened ages of the past.

In addition to the cañons, Arizona is filled with numerous other natural curiosities and scenery, sufficient to keep the explorer in a continued state of wonder and surprise.

The southern portion of the Territory has numerous sugar-loaf mountains, which rise abruptly from the surface of the great plains and valleys to a height of hundreds and thousands of feet, and are called there picachos. Many of them are entirely isolated, and have no connection with any mountain range.

Their formation is a mystery, and a subject of deep thought and study. They may have had originally a connection with other mountains, but the degradation of the connection is so complete, that not a vestige now remains.

An interesting formation is that known as Castle Dome, thirty miles northeast from Yuma. On the highest point of the Colorado River range of mountains, about ten miles east of the river, is a rock formation hundreds of feet square, which, at a distance, looks like a great castle. This can be seen for a hundred miles or more in different directions, and is a noted landmark of the country.

Another noted landmark is the Four Peaks, which are four mountain peaks near Salt River, and but a few miles from Camp McDowell. They rise to a height of several thousand feet, and can be seen for hundreds of miles.

Farther up Salt River is an extensive salt formation through which Salt River runs. It is some one
hundred miles or more above Phœnix. The salt is
so extensive that the whole volume of water in the
river is impregnated with it, rendering it so salt a
stranger can barely drink of it, though in other respects it is clear and pure. To obtain a full idea of
this immense saline formation, one must bear in
mind the fact that the river, where it emerges from
the mountains, has a width of two hundred feet and
a depth of nearly twenty inches, with a swift current. For at least two hundred years there has been
no abatement in the saltness of the water of the
river, which was named the Rio Salido (River of
Salt) over two centuries since, by the early Spanish
and Jesuit explorers.

In different parts of the Territory are peculiar
mountain formations, resembling the thumb of a man,
which are called Thumb Buttes. One of these is a
few miles west from Prescott, and is a conspicuous
object in the mountain scenery of that region.

The grandest mountain in all Arizona is San Francisco Peak, eighty-five miles north of east from Prescott. It rises to an altitude of over thirteen thousand
feet, and is plainly distinguishable at a distance of
over two hundred miles. It rises to a height far above
the timber line, and its hoary head, " rock-ribbed and
ancient as the sun," is considered by the simple Zuñi

Indians to be one end of the earth. The Zuñis live nearly two hundred miles far to the northeast of the mountain, and it is no wonder that they should attach much importance to this great mountain, whose bald crown rises so high above all other mountains, and whose rocky sides are covered with snow for ten months in the year.

The great Tonto Basin is a natural depression in the mountains, midway between Prescott and Camp Apache, where the great Tonto and other creeks rise, and flow south into Salt River. It is fifty miles or more across, and surrounded most of the way by precipitous wall rocks, and almost unapproachable. For many years it was the resort of hostile Apaches, who fled to its recesses where they were in comparative safety. A few renegades yet seek its fastnesses as a secure hiding place from their pursuers. This basin is as yet almost wholly unknown, except to the military, who from time to time have pursued the hostile Indians into its wonderful cañons and gorges.

The Zuñi Lake is near the eastern line of Arizona, some thirty miles from the Milligan Settlement, which is on the upper waters of the Chiquito Colorado River. It is in one of the most desolate regions on the continent, surrounded by bleak, barren, desolate, volcanic mountains, with no outlet, and is nearly one mile across in its widest part. The water is in no place over five feet deep. In the southern part of the lake is a volcanic cone about eighty feet above the surface of the lake, and from this cone there issues a stream of salt water, somewhat impregnated with saltpetre, which flows continually into the lake, keeping up a uniform height. The heat of the sun evaporates the water and leaves the salt as a residuum in a crystallized form.

The depth of the deposit of salt is unknown, but it has been opened over five feet deep, and is found pure at that depth. It is an excellent quality for preserving meat, and for table and other purposes. The hollow cone from which the water issues is two feet in diameter and of great depth. Ropes have been sunk to a depth of nearly one hundred feet without touching bottom.

A load of this salt was brought to Prescott in July, 1876, which sold for five cents per pound. The distance from Prescott to the lake is over two hundred miles. At one point a wagon can approach the lake, and being driven into it, the salt is shoveled up like so much sand or gravel. There is a spring of pure water four hundred yards to the south of the lake, which is the only good drinking water for many miles around.

From time immemorial, the Zuñi Indians have obtained salt from the lake, and they hold it sacred, going there for salt only at stated times and seasons. They do not like to have other tribes or people go there, but now permit the whites to do so.

In the northern and northeastern portions of Arizona are a number of curious and interesting lakes, or, as some of them are called, " wells," of pure fresh water. One near the Navajoe Springs is called Jacob's Well. Another is known as Stoneman's Lake. Several are found near Bill Williams Mountain, and one, which will be briefly described, is about fifty-five miles north of east from Prescott, and is called Montezuma Well.

This well, or lake, is near Beaver Creek, twelve miles northeast from Camp Verde, on the Verde River, and two miles east from Mr. Arnold's ranch or farm. It is in a limestone formation, and on a piece of tableland or mesa, elevated above the creek about one hundred feet. This mesa is level, and its surface is the bare limestone rock, with no bush, tree, or verdure on it. The opening to the well is circular, and as perfect as though made by the hand of man, and is about six hundred feet across. From the surface of the mesa to the water, is seventy feet. The water is clear and pure, and nearly or quite one hundred feet deep. The inner walls of the opening are perpendicular, and access to the water is almost impossible, except on the southeast side, where the walls are partially broken down, and where ladies can approach the water with assistance.

On the northwest side are three or four cave dwellings, about midway between the water and the sur-

face of the mesa. These dwellings are from twelve
to twenty feet across in front, and about the same
depth, and are walled up in front. They were evidently inhabited by the old prehistoric people described in another chapter. The eastern and southeastern borders of the well approach Beaver Creek
within thirty to one hundred feet, and it is separated
from the creek by a rim of the inclosing limestone
rock. This rim of rock was built up with stone
buildings its whole width, and about one hundred
feet in length. The walls of these old buildings are
yet standing to a height of twenty feet in places.

On the southeast side of the well is another old
cave dwelling, which can be explored fully one hundred feet. It is near the surface of the water of the
well, which runs off under the cave and discharges
the water into the creek some two hundred feet to
the south, in a pretty cascade of about one hundred
inches of water.

This stream is continuous the whole year. The
whole surface surrounding the well is strewn with
broken pottery ware of various sizes, forms, and patterns. In walking around the rim of the well, the
limestone rock gives forth a ringing metallic sound,
as though it had been subjected at some former time
to extreme heat. Below the well, on the creek flat,
are two or three dykes of volcanic lava. From all the
surroundings, it is quite evident that the well was at

one time, in the far distant past, the crater of a long
since extinct volcano.   Mr. Arnold, who lives two
miles below, has a small row boat on the lake or well,
in which one can ride across its smooth and glassy
surface, which is ever quiet and unruffled by wind
or storm.

This is a pleasant resort for picnic and other parties from Prescott, Camp Verde, and elsewhere, who
find it exceedingly interesting. Both male and female
visitors can enter the large cave, where, seated on the
limestone slabs of rock, they can enjoy its coolness,
drink of the crystal water, and lunch in the most ap-
proved romantic style.

Some large open-mouthed bottles have been placed
on the shelving rock of the great cave, where visitors
leave their cards with such inscriptions as seem ap-
propriate to the time and place.

Though evidently, as before stated, the crater of
an extinct volcano, future critical examinations by
wise men and savants may determine otherwise.
Whatever the final decision may be, the well is one
of the most interesting of the many natural curiosities of this or any other country, and is worth a trip
across the continent to see.

There are but few thermal springs in Arizona com-
pared to the numbers found in California, and of
these but little is yet satisfactorily known as to their
chemical constituents or curative qualities. Some of

them have been found beneficial in rheumatic and kindred complaints. They may in the future become noted resorts for invalids.

One of the best known is that of the Agua Caliente, near Stanwix Station, ninety-five miles east from Yuma, owned by the Hon. King S. Woolsey.

A series of hot sulphur springs are in the Sulphur Spring Valley, seventy miles east from Tucson. There are others in the Santa Catarina Mountains, and in the Pueblo Viejo Valley, as well as in other localities in the Territory. Future examination, and an analysis of these waters, is necessary to determine as to their value as curative agents.

The foregoing is but a faint and imperfect description of a few of the many natural curiosities found in Arizona, a country so filled with objects of interest, of an all absorbing character, one can never tire in his explorations, and can feast on new and wonderful formations from day to day, and year to year.

16

CHAPTER XXIV.

THE FLORA OF ARIZONA.

THE flora of Arizona approximates in character to that of tropical climates. It would require much time and study, and long continued research, to write up a full description of the flora of the Territory. A brief description was given in a preceding chapter, of timber forests, and the most common wood of the country. Brief mention will now be made of a few only of the numerous floral productions, and of some of their qualities and uses.

A very large proportion of the trees, shrubbery, plants, and flowers of the Territory are literally covered with thorns; so general is this, some wag in a former day in commenting on the Territory asserted, among other objections to the country, that " everything which grew there had a thorn."

Of the cactus family (order Cactaceæ) there are over one hundred varieties. They are of all forms and sizes, from the tiny cross cactus, like two needle points crossed, to the giant cactus tree (the *Cereus giganteus*), which grows to the height of a forest tree. The Cereus giganteus is often found sixty feet in height, with a diameter of three feet. It is supported by ribs of very great strength and toughness. These ribs are from one to two inches wide, about the same distance apart, and extend from the root of the plant to its apex. It is long lived, and when in a green state the interstices between the ribs and the interior part is filled with a dark green substance, resembling a green pumpkin. When the tree dies the whole of it, except the ribs, dries up and dissolves into an impalpable powder, which is blown away. The ribs being strong and elastic are used for covering the adobe houses, on which is put the earth covering in place of shingles or boards. They are also used for many other purposes where strength and durability are required. They often grow to a height of sixty feet without a branch, sometimes having a few which grow out laterally one or two feet, and then turn up like a crooked elbow, and run up parallel with the parent stem. On the apex of both parent stem and the limbs are beautiful clusters of white flowers, which produce a delicious pear-shaped fruit, the size of a common pear, which has the combined flavor of the peach, strawberry, and fig. It is gathered and eaten in great quantities by the Indians, and is highly prized by the whites.

Another variety of the cactus is the Ocotea, so called by the inhabitants of the country. It grows

like a cane to a height of ten to twenty feet, in
bunches of twenty to fifty from one root. The
ocotea is sometimes cut and set out for hedges, making a fence impassable for anything larger than a
small bird. It produces a cluster of bright scarlet
flowers, but no fruit.

Of the Choya cactus there are many varieties.
They grow in bush form, with numerous branches
having long thorny prongs, and have a white flower,
but no fruit.

The common prickly pear cactus (*Cactus opuntia*)
is distributed over the whole Territory. It produces
different colored flowers, and a pear-shaped edible
fruit, having an acid and pleasant taste. The author
counted on one bush, on the eastern declivities of the
Bradshaw Mountains, over one thousand of these
pears.

The barrel cactus resembles the Cereus giganteus,
and grows to an extreme height of ten feet, with a
diameter of nearly two feet. It produces no fruit.

The kind commonly called the nigger head is
round, of the size of a cabbage, and covered with
large, crooked, catlike thorns.

There are many other varieties worthy of description, and which would be interesting to the botanist
and florist.

The maguey plant, of the genus agave, known in
the Mexican States, Arizona, and New Mexico as

the mescal plant, is one of the most useful and important of all the indigenous plants of the country. It grows profusely at certain altitudes in all sections of the Territory. It produces a bulbous like root, partly in, and partly above the ground, which is rich in saccharine matter. These bulbs are from the size of a cabbage to a bushel basket, and when roasted are sweet and delicious. The Indians will live on it for a long time. From the root there grows up large, long, thorny pointed leaves, and from the centre a stalk rises to a height of ten or more feet, having a few branches and a flowering pod which incloses the seed. The juice of the plant when boiled down makes a good syrup. A liquor is made from the plant by distillation, which has the taste and flavor of old Scotch whiskey, and which is the favorite strong drink of the Mexicans.

The fiber of the leaves is strong, and from it ropes are made and used quite extensively among the Indians and Mexicans. A more useful plant would be difficult to find. The Indians at the San Carlos Agency gathered and roasted for use, in 1875, over seventy five thousand pounds of the mescal, and all the Indians of the Territory gather and use it quite extensively.

Another plant, called there the amole, with leaves similar to the mescal, has a bulbous root, which is very valuable as a detergent. It grows to the

height of three feet or more. It is successfully used
for cleansing clothing, and makes a fine wash for the
hair, to which it imparts a soft and glossy appearance.

It grows abundantly in the Territory, and offers
an opportunity for some wide awake, ingenious
Yankee, to make a fortune.

The mesquit tree, before mentioned, is probably a
variety of the acacia, and like it, produces the gum
arabic of commerce. There are two kinds of the
mesquit, both of which produce a bean which is
sweet and nutritious, and which the Indians gather in
large quantities to be eaten either in the green or
dried state. When dried they grind it into a kind
of flour, living on it for months at a time. The bean
is very fattening for all kinds of stock, and is well
liked by horses, cattle, sheep, and hogs. One kind has
a pod much like that of the large string-bean, and
the other, which is called the screw bean, resembles
a bunch of the alder tags and is screw shaped. The
wood of the tree is very hard, excellent for fire-
wood, and used to some extent for wagon felloes and
other work.

It is a very durable wood, and for railroad ties
would equal the lignum-vitæ of tropical climates.
Its botanical name is *Algarobia glandulosa.*

There are many varieties of the pine found growing on the mountains and mountain plateaus of

Arizona, which are good for lumber and timber, which in time will become very useful for building purposes, and especially for timbering and working the numerous mines of the country.

One kind, the common piñon of the country (*Pinus edulis*) bears a large quantity of fruit known as the piñon nut, which is gathered and eaten in great quantities by the natives. The nut is of the size of the common hazel-nut, sweet and edible. Swine fatten on it readily, and other stock eat it with avidity.

There are many herbs and shrubs indigenous to the country possessed of rare medicinal qualities. One kind is much used by the Mexicans for fevers, with the best of results. Two kinds assimilate to the tea plant, and the leaves gathered in a green state make a pleasant and aromatic drink.

Edible berries are not very numerous, yet in the mountains there are varieties of the barberry, whortleberry, strawberry, and a few others.

A large variety of flowering plants grow profusely throughout the Territory, and during each rainy season, there being two in the year, the mountains, hills, valleys, and plains present a beautiful and gorgeous sight.

The blossoming willow is very beautiful, the flower resembling in form and size the honeysuckle. There is a rich field in Arizona for the florist, and the botanist, as yet almost wholly unknown, though several parties have made partial examinations of the Territory, and gathered many choice specimens.

Long months and years could be passed in the Territory, in the examination and classification of the floral products of the country, and in thoroughly studying their properties and uses.

CHAPTER XXV.

ROUTES OF TRAVEL TO ARIZONA.

TO all desiring to go to Arizona, this is a necessary and important subject for consideration.

There are two routes by public conveyance from San Francisco, one by steamer from San Francisco to either San Pedro, Santa Monica, or San Diego. If by Santa Monica or San Pedro, from both those points the Southern Pacific Railroad will be taken at Los Angeles, from fifteen to twenty miles from those ports, and thence by that railroad either to Yuma, to which point the railroad will be completed before the first of July of the present year, or to the nearest point on the Colorado to Ehrenburg, which will be less than 100 miles. By the route to Yuma one can there take the stage of the Southern Pacific Mail Line to Maricopa Wells, Florence, Tucson, and all points in Southern Arizona, connecting at Maricopa Wells with a stage route to Phœnix, and thence by the California and Arizona Stage Company to Wickenburg, Prescott, and all points in the central and northern parts of the Territory. On the Colorado Desert, at

the nearest point to Ehrenburg, the California and
Arizona Stage Company connect with the railroad
semi-weekly, and will soon make daily connections,
crossing the Colorado River at Ehrenburg, and
thence running to Wickenburg, Prescott, and all intermediate points. At Wickenburg a branch line
runs to Phœnix and Florence, at the latter point
connecting with the Southern Pacific Mail Line, and
at Phœnix with stage lines to Camp McDowell east,
and with Maricopa Wells southwest.

Those desiring to visit the beautiful town and har-
bor of San Diego, go to that point by steamer from
San Francisco, and thence by stage on the Southern
Pacific Mail Line to Yuma, and thence by the same
line to other points as before designated.

The distance by stage from San Diego to Yuma
is 200 miles, from Yuma to Maricopa Wells 183, to
Florence 237, to Tucson 300, and to Apache Pass
425 miles.

Emigrants going from California to Arizona will,
with teams and stock, follow nearly on the line indicated from Los Angeles, and if on reaching the Colorado Desert, they desire to go to Mineral Park, Cerbat, Prescott, or elsewhere in the central or northern
parts of the Territory, they will, at or near Indian
Wells, take the northern route, crossing the Colorado
River at Hardyville, where there is an excellent ferry
kept by William M. Hardy, Esq., and thence go to

any of the selected central or northern portions of
the Territory.

The most expeditious route from San Francisco is
by the Southern Pacific Railroad, by which route one
can (by the first of July, 1877) enter Arizona at
Yuma in less than three days, and at Ehrenburg by
stage connection, as before stated, in the same time.

Several northern routes from Nevada and Eastern
California centre and cross the Colorado River at
Stone's Ferry, thence pursuing a southerly course
for eighty miles to Mineral Park, and thence to Prescott and elsewhere as desirable. Many immigrants
with stock come in on this route, which is very favorable during the winter.

Those desiring to go to Arizona from the southwestern States, from any point between St. Louis and
New Orleans, will take any one of the many routes
that pass through the Indian Territory and Texas;
and if desiring to go to the northern part of the Territory, either to Prescott, the Chiquito Colorado Valley, or elsewhere, will make their way to Santa Fé,
or Albuquerque, from which points good emigrant
roads lead west to all points. If desiring to go to
Tucson, or Southern Arizona, they will intersect the
Southern Pacific Stage and Mail line at Mesilla, on
the Rio Grande River, from which point by stage it
is but 350 miles to Tucson. This is a good stage
route, as well as an excellent one for immigrants,
with teams and stock.

Immigrants from north of St. Louis, including all the northwestern, northern, and eastern States, can obtain a good outfit at Kansas City, Topeka, and many other points to the west of those cities on the line of the Atchison, Topeka, and Santa Fé Railroad, or on the line of the Kansas Pacific, or Denver and Rio Grande railroads, and from any point selected, find a good road with wood and water to Santa Fé and Albuquerque, and thence a good route via the Chiquito Colorado to Prescott, and all points in Northern Arizona.

Those going from Utah, or from the east, who go by railroad to Salt Lake City, can continue by rail-road to Nephi, which is less than 500 miles from Prescott. This road is being pushed forward with vigor, and in a few years, at farthest, will reach Prescott, and thence, as supposed, be continued on to the Port of Guaymas, on the Gulf of California.

There is a certainty now, that in a few years at the farthest, Arizona will be traversed by railroads in all directions, her rich mines be fully developed, and a career of prosperity opened which has long been earnestly looked for by her citizens. With the completion of railroads, and the development of mines, all other industries will prosper. Her rich agricultural lands will be settled and tilled, her millions of acres of grazing lands will be covered by numerous flocks of sheep and herds of cattle; manufactories will be established, of mills and machinery of all kinds, of woolen goods, of sugar refineries, of hemp and cordage, and all other kinds needed; brisk and prosperous towns and cities will spring into existence, and in less than a decade of years, a prosperous, wide-awake, and energetic American population will have centered in her borders, and she will be knocking at the doors of Congress for admission into the Union, where she will become a bright star in the galaxy of free and independent States of the great American Union.

This picture is not overdrawn. Arizona has not only the possibilities, she has also the probabilities which point unerringly to an early fulfillment of all, and more than all, which has been said of her in these pages; and when in the coming time her history shall be written, what has herein been said will have been fulfilled.

CHAPTER XXVI.

DISTANCES FROM POINT TO POINT.

FROM YUMA.

	Miles.
To San Diego, California, west	200
Castle Dome, on Colorado River, north	35
Ehrenburg, on Colorado River, north	135
Colorado River Reservation, on Colorado River, north	220
Aubrey, on Colorado River, north	245
Needles, on Colorado River, north.	285
Camp Mohave, on Colorado River, north	325
Hardyville, on Colorado River, north	337
Colorado Cañon, on Colorado River, north	400
Callville, on Colorado River, north	460
Stone's Ferry, on Colorado River, north	510
Mouth of River, Colorado River, south	175
Gila City, in Gila Valley, east	22
Oatman Flat, in Gila Valley, east	118
Maricopa Wells, in Gila Valley, east	191
Pima Village, in Gila Valley, east	203
Florence, in Gila Valley, east	237
Tucson, in Santa Cruz Valley, east	300
Tres Alimos, in San Pedro Valley, east	350
Apache Pass, Camp Bowie, east	425
Ralston, New Mexico, east	475
Silver City, New Mexico, east	525
Mesilla, New Mexico, east	645

From Ehrenburg.

	Miles.
To connections with Southern Pacific Railroad, west . .	100
San Bernardino, California, west	230
Wickenburg, Arizona, east	140
Prescott, Arizona, northeast	220

From Mineral Park.

To Hardyville, on Colorado River, southwest	35
Cerbat, south	6
McCracken Mine, south	100
Greenwood, east of south	100
Hackberry Mine, east	35
Stone's Ferry of Colorado River, north	80
Hualapai Mountains, southeast	30
Cottonwood Station, east	51
Anvil Rock, east	81
Oaks and Willows, east	90
Camp Hualapai, east	103
Williamson's Valley, east	121
Prescott, east	141

From Prescott.

To Williamson's Valley, west	20
Mineral Park, west	141
Hackberry Mine, west	110
Chino Valley, north	22
Agua Frio Valley, east	15
Camp Verde, east	42
San Francisco Mountain, east of north	85
Nephi, Utah Southern Railroad, northeast . . .	500
Black Cañon, southeast	52
Peck Mine, southeast	30
Fredericks Mill, on Hassayampa, southeast . . .	10
Aztlan Mill, Peck Co., south	6

Miles.

Walnut Grove on air line, south	15
Camp McDowell, east of south	92
Wickenburg, south	82
Hardyville, on Colorado River, west	180
Ehrenburg, on Colorado River, southwest	220
Sunset Crossing, on Chiquito Colorado, north of east .	132
Stoneman's Lake, north of east	75
Montezuma Well, north of east	55
Phœnix, south	142
Florence, south	192
Silver King Mine, east of south	190
Tucson, south	267
Apache Pass, Camp Bowie, southeast	392

FROM WICKENBURG.

To Prescott, north	82
Ehrenburg, west	140
Phœnix, south	60
Florence, south	110
Camp McDowell, southeast	95
Tucson, south	185
Mineral Park, northwest	225
Hardyville, northwest	260
Yuma, via Ehrenburg and Colorado River, southwest .	265
Yuma, via Phœnix and Maricopa Wells, southwest .	286

FROM PHŒNIX.

To Wickenburg, north	60
Prescott, north	142
Camp McDowell, east	35
Florence, south	50
Tucson, south	125
Yuma, via Maricopa Wells, west	226
Maricopa Wells, southwest	35

From Florence.

	Miles.
To Phœnix, north	50
Prescott, north	192
Wickenburg, north	110
Silver King Mine, northeast	35
Globe District, Pinal Mountains, northeast	75
Sanford, west	6
Casa Grande, west	12
Pima Villages, west	34
Maricopa Wells, west	46
Yuma, west	237
San Diego, California, west	437
Tucson, southeast	75

From Tucson.

To Florence, northwest	75
Yuma, west	300
San Diego, California, west	500
Sonora line, south	75
Ostrich Mine, west of south	85
Young America Copper Mines, west	50
Santa Rita Mountains, south	65
Trench Mine, south	75
Mowry Mine, south	85
Tres Alimos, on San Pedro, east	50
Apache Pass, Camp Bowie, east	125
Silver City, New Mexico, east	225
Mesilla, on Rio Grande, New Mexico, east	345
Camp Grant, north of east	110
Pueblo Viejo, north of east	150
San Carlos, Indian Agency, northeast	160
Camp Apache, White Mountains, northeast	225

17

The distance from Prescott and Tucson to St. Louis, Missouri, is about fifteen hundred miles.

All other mining camps and settlements can be easily reached from some of the places mentioned.

CHAPTER XXVII.

REFERENCES AND GENERAL REMARKS.

FOR the benefit and convenience of those desiring information respecting **Arizona**, its soil, climate, productions, minerals, general business prospects, etc., etc., a list will be given below of some of the leading business men and citizens of the principal towns, to whom communications may be addressed, and whose answers may be relied on for correct and reliable information.

Address at Yuma, A. T.: Col. James M. Barney; David Neahr; Hon. J. M. Redondo; Capt. I. Polhemus, Jr.; A. J. Finlay; Judge Porter; C. H. Brinlay; Judge Alexander; Editor of "Sentinel."

At Castle Dome, Yuma Co., A. T.: Wm. P. Miller, Esq.

At Ehrenburg, Yuma Co., A. T.: Chas. Vandevere, Agt. J. M. Barney; J. Goldwater & Bro.; J. M. Castenado; E. O. Grant, Agt. C. & A. Stage Co.

At Colorado River Reservation, Yuma Co., A. T.: Col. Wm. E. Morford, Agt.

At McCracken Mine, Mohave Co., A. T.: A. Bateman, Supt.; D. B. Pierce, Asst.; Joseph S. Currie, Assayer.

At Greenwood, Mohave Co., A. T.: Joseph Mc-Cracken; Col. Buell; A. Cady.

At Cerbat, Mohave Co., A. T.: Wm. Corey, P. M.; Sheriff Comstock.

At Mineral Park, Mohave Co., A. T.: Alder Randall, P. M.; Messrs. Breon & Spear; Hon. James Bull; Capt. Welbourne; T. J. Christie; Hon. Mr. Wood.

At Hackberry Mine, Mohave Co., A. T.: Hon. A. E. Davis; Judge Wm. Towle.

At Oaks and Willows, Yavapai Co., A. T.: G. S. Smith, P. M.

At Williamson Valley, Yavapai Co., A. T.: Stephen Breon.

At Prescott, Arizona Territory: Col. C. P. Head & Co.; L. Bashford & Co.; Hon. John G. Campbell; Hon. Geo. D. Kendall; Hon. John P. Rush; Hon. Gideon Brooks; Hon. John H. Marion; Hon. C. C. Bean; Messrs. Bowers & Richards; Wm. C. Foster, Esq.; Hon. C. A. Luke; Hon. E. G. Peck; Dr. McCandles; Judge H. H. Carter; Sheriff Bowers; J. C. Behan, Esq.; Editors "Miner;" Editors "Enterprise."

At Agua Frio P. O., Yavapai Co., A. T.: Postmaster; Nathan Bowers, Esq.

At Camp Verde, Yavapai Co., A. T.: Major Brayton; Hon. Wm. Head.

At Walnut Grove, Yavapai Co., A. T.: Hon. E. G. Peck; C. A. Morrison; A. Cullumber, Esq.; Capt. S. Bartlett; Geo. Hogle, Assayer; Geo. Jackson, Esq.; J. O. Wood.

At Wickenburg, Yavapai Co., A. T.: Dr. J. H. Pierson; H. Wickenburg, Esq.; Dr. Jones; Wm. Smith.

At Phœnix, Maricopa Co., A. T.: Hon. John T. Smith; Hon. King S. Woolsey; Hon. Granville Oury; Major C. H. Vail; Wm. B. Hellings.

At Maricopa Wells, A. T.: James A. Moore, Esq.

At Hayden's Ferry, Maricopa Co., A. T.: Hon. Chas. T. Hayden.

At Florence, Pinal Co., A. T.: Messrs. Collingwood & Hammerslag; Wm. Long; Judge Ruggles; Judge J. D. Walker; Hon. P. B. Brady; J. Clark, Atty.

At Tucson, Arizona Territory: Messrs. Tully, Ochoa, & Co.; Messrs. Lord & Williams; Hon. Hiram S. Stevens, Delegate in Congress; Judge French, U. S. Supreme Judge of A. T.; Dr. J. C. Handy; Gov. A. P. K. Safford; Hon. John Wasson, Editor "Citizen;" J. H. Archibald; Hon. John S. Wood; Right Rev. Bishop Salpointe; Messrs. Zeckendorf & Co.; M. I. Jacobs & Co.; S. Drachman & Co.; T. Wellisch; E. N. Fish & Co.; Hon. Mr. Bennett.

At Camp Bowie, Apache Pass, Pima Co., A. T.: Hon. Mr. De Long ; Capt. C. B. McLellan; Capt. J. Jefferds.

At Tres Alimos, San Pedro River, Pima Co., A. T.: H. C. Hooker, Esq.; Hon. Mr. Montgomery; Mr. Dunbar.

At Camp Grant, A. T.: Major C. E. Compton, Commandant ; Hon. Geo. A. Stevens.

At Safford P. O., Pueblo Viejo Valley, Pima Co., A. T.: J. E. Bailey, P. M.; Isaac Clanton ; Mr. Kirkland.

At San Carlos Agency, Pima Co., A. T.: J. P. Clum, Agt. ; M. A. Sweeney, Clerk.

At Camp Apache, White Mts., Yavapai Co., A. T.: Capt. F. D. Ogilby, Commandant ; Capt. Wm. S. Worth ; Mr. James, Post Trader.

At Chiquito Colorado, Yavapai Co., A. T.: Chas. Franklin, J. P.; S. & M. Barth ; Mr. Milligan.

At Silver King Mine, Pinal Co., A. T.: Judge Anderson ; A. Mason, Supt. ; H. Kearsing, Assayer.

At Globe District, Pinal Co., A. T.: Chas. Brown ; E. M. Pearce ; Messrs Garrish & Co. ; Mr. William-son ; Mr. Newman.

All of the gentlemen named in the foregoing list are good and reliable men. The number could have been increased to an indefinite extent, but the names given are representative gentlemen in military, civil, and private life, and represent all parts of the Territory. Of the hundreds and **thousands in** different parts of the Union who are making inquiries respecting Arizona and its climate, productions, etc., those who do not obtain that specific information desired, in these pages, are referred to the gentlemen named, who will no doubt be pleased to answer all inquiries respecting the country.

While the author has been earnest and untiring in his endeavor to let the people of the United States, and the world, know all about Arizona, and has given to the public during the past three years a series of articles through the press, numbering in all over five hundred, descriptive of its climate, soil, productions, scenery, minerals, etc., etc., endeavoring in an honorable and truthful manner to draw attention to, and assist in its permanent development, and while believing it to possess stores of mineral wealth, unequaled by any other country, he deems it his duty to caution those desiring to emigrate there, against being over sanguine. All new countries have their dark sides, and many and serious difficulties the emigrant will meet with, which must be overcome with will, energy, and perseverance.

Fortunes cannot be made in Arizona, or elsewhere, without work, and hard work too. Mines of wonderful wealth permeate and traverse all the mountain ranges, but the hardy and untiring prospector must undergo weeks, months, and sometimes years, of toil and fatigue, before a choice location will be found, and when discovered, it will take generally long, long months to develop and uncover its hidden treasures. During all this time, one must be content to live on scant and simple fare, must sleep most of the time on mother earth, with but a blanket for a covering, must work early and late, and at times suffer untold hardships.

If the hopeful youth, or matured man, can do all this without losing courage, and will keep clear from drinking and gambling saloons, and other vices, he can in a few years acquire a competency, perhaps great wealth.

Arizona wants men of energy, of perseverance and determination, men of muscle, men of brains, men of wealth, to assist in developing her great resources. All such will be welcomed to her borders by her large hearted, wide-awake citizens, who are ready to assist and advise those who may desire to make the country their home. She throws wide open her doors to immigrants from all parts of the world.

To the capitalist who desires to invest his money in rich mines, which well managed will pay large dividends for many years to come, she says come and assist in her development. Untold millions are here hoarded up for your and your country's use.

To the young man, full of honest day's work, who desires a new field for labor, and can resist temptation, and maintain his manhood, and who has a laudable ambition for the future, Arizona sends greeting, and bids you a hearty welcome to her borders, where in a few years by honest labor you can secure independence, and a fortune for old age.

To the broken down in health, whose every breath is drawn in agony and pain, who have suffered a thousand deaths during long years of suffering and sickness, the balmy skies and pure atmosphere of Arizona will greet you in winter to a mild and balmy climate in her great plains and valleys, and in summer the pure and rarefied atmosphere of her mountain plateaus will be breathed with pleasure, and life will again become a blessing to you, instead of a curse.

Stock raisers will here find an almost unlimited range for sheep, cattle, and horses, where millions can be kept and fattened on the rich grasses of the valleys, mountains, and plains, with but little care, and at a trifling expense.

To farmers, horticulturists, and pomologists, Arizona presents a rich field for operations. Hundreds and thousands of these classes could in a few years accumulate a competency in either of these branches of business, and build up beautiful homes for old age.

Skilled mechanics and laborers of all kinds are wanted. Towns and cities are to be built, mills and manufactories are to be erected, and good workmen must be had for the purpose, to whom good wages and constant employment will be given.

Hundreds of families have emigrated to Arizona the past two years, who are well pleased with the country and climate, and thousands more are wanted to assist in building up churches, schools, and good society. The dangers of Indian warfare, of murders, pillage, and robbery, are virtually over, and fathers and mothers need have no fear for themselves or their little ones. The domination of savage life has ended, and that of civilization has usurped its place, bringing in its train the blessings of peace, security, and prosperity. Therefore we say to families, come to Arizona, where the skies are ever bright, where disease and sickness are almost unknown, where nature's bountiful gifts await you in a thousand varied forms of beauty and grandeur.

Like all newly settled countries, there is a great disproportion between the different sexes, the male outnumbering the female, as five or ten to one.

This fact alone calls for the emigration of large numbers of females to the Territory, where constant and remunerative employment would be given to good help. Cooks, chamber-maids, seamstresses, teachers, etc., are wanted, for which several employments from thirty to fifty dollars and often one hundred dollars a month are paid.

Recognizing the fact that no community, or country, can ever enter upon its highest state of prosperity, refinement, or happiness without the aid and assistance of woman, Arizona and her citizens would welcome the advent of large numbers of the true, the pure, the good, of the superabundant females of other portions of the Union, and would give them a welcome such as goddesses might envy.

CHAPTER XXVIII.

PRICES OF PRODUCE, PROVISIONS, LABOR, ETC.
REMARKS.

PRICES are given in greenbacks, as that is the currency of the Territory, though on and near the Colorado River a specie basis prevails to some extent: —

Wheat, per pound	$0.02½ @ $0.04
Barley, per pound	.02½ @ .04
Corn, per pound	.02½ @ .04
Flour, per 100 pounds	10.00 @ 12.00
Bacon and ham, per pound	.30 @ .40
Pork, per pound	.25 @ .30
Beef, per pound	.15 @ .20
Venison, per pound	.15 @ .20
Potatoes, sweet, per pound	.10 @ .15
Potatoes, Irish, per pound	.05 @ .10
Garden vegetables, per pound	.05 @ .10
Mutton, per pound	.10 @ .15
Coffee, per pound	.40 @ .75
Sugar, per pound	.20 @ .30
Beans, per pound	.08 @ .10
Board, per week	8.00 @ 10.00
Lumber, per M	25.00 @ 50.00
Day laborers, per day	2.50 @ 3.00

Blacksmiths, per day	4.00 @	6.00
Carpenters, per day	4.00 @	6.00
Masons and Bricklayers, per day . . .	5.00 @	8.00
Miners, per day	3.00 @	5.00
Farm hands, with board, per month . . .	30.00 @	50.00
Herders, with board, per month	30.00 @	40.00
Teamsters, with board, per month . . .	40.00 @	50.00
Cooks, with board, per month	30.00 @	60.00
Nurses, with board, per day	3.00 @	5.00
Teachers, per month	50.00 @	100.00
House help, with board, per month . . .	20.00 @	40.00
Skilled Machinists and Millwrights, per month .	100.00 @	200.00
Apples, per pound	.05 @	.10
Peaches, per pound	.06 @	.15
Grapes, per pound	.10 @	.15
Pears, per pound	.06 @	.10
Melons, each	.25 @	1.00

With the present price of lumber and material for
building, it costs about thirty per cent. more to build
than in the States east of the Rocky Mountains.
Houses and stores can be rented at about the same
comparative rates as it would cost to build. Scores
of families on arriving in the Territory live for
months in tents or under wagon covers, until they
have time and opportunity to select a permanent
home and erect suitable buildings. The climate is
so mild and pure they suffer no ills or danger from
sickness by so doing. Many who came to the Territory in its early days lived for years in this way,
buoyed up by the hope that in a few years a home
and a competency would be obtained.

In most instances that hope has been more than fulfilled, and though harassed for years by roving bands of the savage Apaches, stock driven off, and crops destroyed, most of the early settlers are now above want, and have homes, houses, and lands, which will compare favorably with those of the Northern and Eastern States.

The foregoing brief description of Arizona, of its soil, climate, and productions; of its minerals and mines; of its prehistoric ruins and grand scenery, is given to the public with the hope that it will attract that attention which its importance demands, and assist to some extent in hastening the time when the Territory will be filled with a numerous and happy people, and when Arizona will become what nature has destined her to be, the *coming country of the continent.*

ALPHABETICAL INDEX.

Accidental Mine, 104.
Adamsville, 153.
Agricultural lands, 42–53.
Agua Frio P. O., 260.
Agua Supai Indians, 169.
Albany Mine, 83.
American Flag Mine, 74.
Amole plant, 245.
Animals, birds, fish, etc., 221–225.
Antelope, or Rich Hill, 64, 65.
Athens Mine, 121.
Arizona, general description of, 13–16.
Arizona flora, 242.
Arizona mines, total, 135.
Aubrey, 147.

Black Snake Mine, 85.
Black Cañon Mines, 110.
Black Warrior Mine, 100.
Blue Cap Mine, 117.
Blue Dick, and other mines, 84.
Bradshaw Basin, 97.
Bradshaw Mountains, 91, 94, 97.

Cactus of Arizona, 242–244.
California and Arizona stage line, 204.
Camp Apache, 213, 217, 262.
Camp Bowie, 216, 262.
Camp Grant, 217, 262.
Camp Lowell, 216.
Camp McDowell, 216.
Camp Mohave, 216.
Camp Thomas, 217.
Camp Verde, 215, 261.
Cañada de Oro, 66.
Casa Grande, 180–182.

Castle Dome, 145, 234, 259.
Castle Dome Mines, 67, 68.
Cerbat, 76, 146, 260.
Cerbat Mountain Mines, 75, 260.
Cereus giganteus, 242, 243.
Cerro Colorado Mine, 131.
Chiquito Colorado, 39, 262.
Chiquito Colorado Valley, 44.
Chimuehueva Indians, 156.
Chloride Flat Mines, 81.
"Citizen," Tucson, 154.
Clifton Copper Mines, 112, 139.
Climate, etc., 27–31.
Coal, 109.
Cocopah Indians, 156.
Colorado River, 35.
Colorado River Indian Reservation, 259.
Colorado Steam Navigation Co., 208–210.
Conner Mine, 85.
Counties and towns, 143–155.

Davis Mine, 102.
Dean Mine, 74.
Del Pasco Mine, 96.
Diana and Pink Eye Mines, 86.
Distances in Arizona, 254–258.

Ehrenburg, 63, 145, 255, 259.
Emma Mine, 131.
Empire Mine, 83.
"Enterprise," Prescott, 149.

Fawn Mine, 111.
First exploration and settlement of Arizona, 17.
Florence, 152, 257, 261.

Fontenoy Mine, 76.
Fort Whipple, 215.
Fort Yuma, 217.
Four Peaks, 234.

George Mine, 111.
Gila River, 37.
Gila Valley, 44.
Globe Copper Mine, 115.
Globe Mining District, 115–119, 262.
Grazing lands, 54–56.
Greenwood, 146, 255, 260.
Gretna Mine, 96.

Hackberry, 255, 260.
Hackberry Mine, 87, 90.
Hardyville, 147.
Hassayampa Placers, 65.
Hayden's Ferry, 261.
Hayden's Mills, 151.
Health, 27, 31.
Helen Mine, 117.
Hitchcock Mines, 105.
Hualapai Indians, 160.
Hualapai Mountains, 48, 74, 75.
Hualapai Valley, 52.

Idlewild Mine, 96.
Independence Mines, 84.
Index Mine, 80.
Indian scouts, 215, 217.
Indian reservations, and remarks, 170–176.
Indian tribes, 156–166.
Indians, total in Arizona, 170.

Keystone Mine, 79.
Kit Carson Mine, 107.

Laporte Mine, 81.
Lone Star Mine, 79.
Lynx Creek, etc., placers, 65.

Maguey plant, 244.
Maricopa County, 114, 151, 152.
Maricopa County Mines, 114.
Maricopa Wells, 152, 261.
Maricopa Indians, 160.
McCracken Hill, 147.

McCracken Mine, 70, 147, 260.
Mesquit tree, 59, 246.
Metallic Accident Mine, 80.
Military Department of Arizona, 215.
Mineral Park Mines, 75, 79.
Mineral Park, 146, 250, 255, 260.
"Miner," Prescott, 148.
Mines and Mining, 61–136.
Mines — placers, 62–67.
Mines — lodes, etc., 67–136.
Mines, total in Arizona, 135.
Mineral belts — suggestions, etc., 137–142.
Mocking-bird Mine, 77.
Mohave County, 48, 51, 69, 146.
Mohave County Mines, 69–91.
Mohave Indians, 156–160.
Montezuma Well, 238.
Moqui Indians, 168.
Mormon settlements, 150.
Mountains of Arizona, 32–34.
Mowry Mine, 126.

Natural curiosities, 229–241.
Navajo Indians, 165.
Newspapers, 211.

Oaks and Willows, 260.
Old missions, 18, 21.
Old Mine, 132.
Oro Plata Mine, 78.
Oriental Mine, 84.
Ostrich Mine, 132.

Painted Rocks, 178.
Papago Indians, 162, 163.
Peacock Mountain Mines, 87, 90.
Peck Mine, 97, 99.
Pennsylvania Mine, 85.
Phœnix, 151, 152, 256, 261.
Picacho Mine, 124.
Pike, and other mines, 121.
Pima County, 153.
Pima County Mines, 122.
Pima Indians, 160.
Pima villages, 162.
Pinal County, 115, 152.
Pinal County Mines, 115–121.
Pinal Silver Mining Co., 94.

Placer Mines, 61–67.
Placeritas, 65.
Planchas de plata, 116.
Planet, 147.
Planet Copper Mine, 69.
Poland, and other mines, 105.
Population, etc., 143.
Pot-holes, etc., 63.
Prehistoric ruins, 177.
Prescott, 148, 149, 249, 255, 260.
Prices of provisions, labor, etc., 268.
Pueblo Viejo Valley, 45.

Quajate Mountains, 122.
Quaker Mine, 85.

Railroads and stage routes, 200.
References and remarks, 259.
Reptiles, etc., 226.
Rescue Mine, 117.
Rich Hill, 64.
Rivers of Arizona, 35.
Rose Bud and Porter Mines, 84.
Routes of travel to Arizona, 249.

Safford, 262.
Salt formations, 235.
Salt River, 38, 43, 45.
Salvador Mine, 107.
San Carlos Agency, 163, 262.
San Francisco Mountains, 32, 33, 235.
San Pedro Valley, 47.
San Simon Valley, 50.
San Xavier del Bac Mission Church, 19, 21.
Santa Cruz Valley, 46.
Santa Rita Mountains, 66, 128.
Santa Rita Placers, 66.
Schenectady Mine, 83.
Schools and education, 196.
Schuylkill Mine, 83.
Sea Serpent Lode, 131.
Senator Mine, 101.
"Sentinel," Yuma, 144.
She-rum Peak, 80, 86.
Sheep raising, 55, 56.
Silver Belt Mine, 106.
Silver Flake Mine, 107.

Silver King Mine, 119, 262.
Silver Mountain District, 122.
Silver Prince Mine, 99.
Sixty-three Mine, 76.
Southern Pacific Mail Line, 202.
St. Gertrude de Tabac, 18.
Stockton Hill Mines, 77.
Sulphur Springs Valley, 50.
Swilling Mine, 110.
Sunday-school Mine, 84.
Surprise Mine, 121.

Telegraphs, 213.
Thurman Mine, 96.
Tiger Mine and lode, 95.
Timber, 57.
Tip Top Mine, 111.
Tonto Basin, 109.
Trench Mine, 125.
Tres Alimos, 262.
Tucson, 18, 153–155, 257, 258, 261.

Virginia Mine, 85.
Vulture Mine, 92.

Wallace Mine, 100.
Walnut Grove, 261.
War Eagle Mine, 97.
War Eagle Mine No. 2, 97.
Weaver Gulch placers, 47–48, 64.
White Mountain Indian Reservation, etc., 64.
Wickenburg, 93, 150, 249, 256, 261.
Williamson Valley, 260.
Wood, 57.
Wool, etc., 55.

Yavapai County, 48, 64, 91, 147.
Yavapai County Mines, 92.
Young America Copper Mines, etc., 123.
Yuma, 143, 259.
Yuma County, 67, 143.
Yuma County Mines, 67.
Yuma, distances from, 254.
Yuma Indians, 157.

Zuni Indians, 166.
Zuni Lake, 236.

www.ingramcontent.com/pod-product-compliance
Lightning Source LLC
Chambersburg PA
CBHW030340270326
41926CB00009B/903